Surviving a
Shark Attack
(on Land)

ALSO BY DR. LAURA SCHLESSINGER

In Praise of Stay-at-Home Moms

Stop Whining, Start Living

The Proper Care and Feeding of Marriage

Bad Childhood—Good Life

Ten Stupid Things Women Do to Mess Up Their Lives

How Could You Do That?!:
The Abdication of Character, Courage, and Conscience

Ten Stupid Things Men Do to Mess Up Their Lives

The Ten Commandments:
The Significance of God's Laws in Everyday Life

Stupid Things Parents Do to Mess Up Their Kids

Ten Stupid Things
Couples Do to Mess Up Their Relationships

The Proper Care and Feeding of Husbands

Woman Power

CHILDREN'S TITLES

Why Do You Love Me?

But I Waaannt It!

Growing Up Is Hard

Where's God?

Surviving a Shark Attack (on Land)

Overcoming Betrayal and
Dealing with Revenge

Dr. Laura Schlessinger

HARPER **LUXE**

An Imprint of HarperCollinsPublishers

HarperCollins books may be purchased for educational, business, or sales promotional use. For information please write: Special Markets Department, HarperCollins Publishers, 10 East 53rd Street, New York, NY 10022.

FIRST HARPERLUXE EDITION

HarperLuxe™ is a trademark of HarperCollins Publishers

Library of Congress Cataloging-in-Publication Data is available upon request.

ISBN: 978-0-06-200246-4

11 12 13 14 ID/RRD 10 9 8 7 6 5 4 3 2 1

The real problem is in the hearts and minds of men. It is not a problem of physics but of ethics. It is easier to denature plutonium than to denature evil from the spirit of man.

—ALBERT EINSTEIN

Contents

Contents

Surviving a Shark Attack (on Land)

Introduction

There is no explanation
for evil. It must be looked
upon as a necessary part of
the order of the universe.
To ignore it is childish,
to bewail it is senseless.

—W. Somerset Maugham

I have written twelve adult books. The genesis of each and every one of them was the sense I got on my radio show of what was happening in our society that I felt a driving need to respond to. This is true from my first publication, *Ten Stupid Things Women Do to Mess Up Their Lives*, almost a decade and a half ago, to the most recent, *In Praise of Stay-at-Home Moms*, with *The Proper Care and Feeding of Husbands* somewhere after the middle.

This book is different. This book is about betrayal and its aftermath. The genesis of this book is my personal rage. This book was to be—when I conjured it up early in 2009—an act of revenge. I have always said on my radio program that I absolutely adore the concept of revenge . . . and I mean that with every fiber of my body. It is just nigh impossible to exact revenge without being immoral, illegal, or fattening. Damn.

I love the short story by Edgar Allan Poe entitled "The Cask of Amontillado." Here's a taste of my desire from his first paragraph: "The thousand injuries of Fortunato I had borne as I best could; but when he ventured upon insult, I vowed revenge. You, who so well know the nature of my soul, will not suppose, however, that I gave utterance to a threat. At length I would be avenged; this was a point definitively settled—but the very definitiveness with which it was resolved, precluded the idea of risk. I must not only punish, but punish with impunity. A wrong is unredressed when retribution overtakes its redresser. It is equally unredressed when the avenger fails to make himself felt as such to him who has done the wrong."

Yeah, baby!

One of my betrayers is dead—and that makes me mad. I wish him alive and well so that he can experience the profound pain of knowing that his attempts at assassination ultimately failed, and I prevailed. Imagine . . . being angry enough to wish someone alive versus dead! He was once a mentor and—I thought—a dear friend. I did realize his insecurities were a major part of his personality, but he'd been kind and supportive and was quite witty and interesting. I was in my twenties, with not much life experience to make me more wary. As he aged and his career waned, he turned mean. To jump-start renewed media awareness of him, he trotted around to radio programs and so-called journalists to say disgusting things about me and sold thirty-year-old pictures of me in the nude to *Hustler*. The photos with a sweet expression and bottom covered were indeed me, but disgusting pictures appropriate for *Hustler*, bottom uncovered, were manufactured. These pictures are all over the Internet and will be so for the rest of my life. That betrayal keeps on giving.

Saturday Night Live used a comedian to play my minor son discovering these photos.

In real life, my son had to deal with this in school.

This person got his fifteen minutes of infamy . . . and then went back into oblivion. Meanwhile, the idea that a "conservative" commentator had posed in the nude turned into a media shark frenzy. This was a large attempt to diminish me in the eyes of the public so that my messages would be dismissed. More than that, on a personal level he took a private and innocent moment from decades before and made it public and ugly. It was humiliating, and made my life hell. That betrayal cut deep, yet there was nothing I could do about it except defend myself and my reputation.

We can come to look upon deaths of our enemies with as much regret as we feel for those of our friends, namely, when we miss their existence as witnesses to our success.

—Arthur Schopenhauer

This book is in part autobiographical, but I will not "be betrayed and tell" by naming names. However, I intend to be reasonably open about my experiences and the pain they caused. While the motivation for this book was my own accumulated and finally exploded pain and fury, the ultimate goal of these writings is to commiserate with you all, as there is no one out there who hasn't experienced betrayals that have resulted in humiliation, pain, and loss of reputation, employment, family, or friends, as well as physical illness resulting from the stress.

Betrayal seems to be a universal and eternal reality of the nature of human beings. We barely get into Genesis when one brother, in a fit of sibling rivalry over a perception of God's favor, kills the other brother. Biblical human history starts with Eve betraying God and suckering Adam into a bite of forbidden fruit. Adam then betrays Eve by throwing her under the bus, making her take responsibility for his action in munching what he shouldn't.

Whether or not you look at biblical writings as history or metaphor, we are left with the same conclusion: betrayal seems an inevitable, vicious, devastating, horrific part of the human condition.

I was sitting one summer day with my dear friend Sheridan Rosenberg while she was relating to me a gut-wrenching situation of betrayal by a girlfriend she was attempting to survive. She said, "There is a reason Dante made betrayal the deepest level of hell."

I had completely forgotten that, and I quickly went to my library. The ninth (and deepest) circle of hell is where sins of betrayal are punished, in a sea of ice fanned frigid by the six wings of the huge, three-faced, fanged and weeping Lucifer! In Dante's underworld, sinners face a descending vortex of horrendous consequences for all eternity depending on their sins. The lustful are perpetually blown about in a whirlwind; the violent boil in a torrent of blood. But betrayers alone are at the bottom, forever tormented by the angel who betrayed God: Lucifer.

At first, assuming there is such a postlife format, I was thrilled to imagine that the people who betrayed my trust, friendship, affection, and loyalty would have to wear thick mittens forever. Then I wondered why betrayers would be the most tortured . . . even more than murderers.

I concluded that betrayals are frightening, destructive, painful, humiliating, demoralizing, and so very, very hard to repair. Betrayals undermine people, relationships (marriages and families), institutions (churches, schools, businesses, government, politics)— everything. The entire fabric of humanity depends upon people depending upon each other for their word, honesty, and loyalty.

Perhaps when a person is betrayed, it is worse than death. In death they no longer suffer the slings and arrows of outrageous antagonisms. While betrayed, they live to suffer the torturous consequences of the betraying. Think about most "scary movies" in which evil is shown resurging (unbeknownst to the protagonists who have struggled to conquer and destroy it). Evil has a lot of power and resilience.

Yes, evil has immense power—and betrayals are evil—because evil has no rules of engagement. Evil has no morals or values to monitor or measure its actions, evil enjoys recognizing the pain it has caused, evil feeds off confrontation, and evil persists ultimately because most people won't stand up to it. Worried about being next in the crosshairs, they deny the existence, potency, or significance of a betrayal because it hasn't touched them—yet.

So it is the fear, weakness, selfishness, and cowardice of onlookers that permits evil behavior to persist.

Both justice and vengeance are difficult to attain. We can't count on "What goes around comes around," or any such palliatives. Open any book on religion,

In the end, we will remember
not the words of our enemies,
but the silence of our friends.

—Martin Luther King, Jr.

psychology, and philosophy, and you will read sub-limely mushy stuff about making friends out of ene-mies. I can't for the life of me conjure up the desire to become intimate with and trust people capable of cold-blooded, calculated, destructive, hateful mean-ness. That just makes no sense to me—unless it is to beguile them into submission by imagining a friend-ship that is there only out of expediency or self-defense.

So what do we do with those who have crossed the line of disagreement or disapproval into blatant ugli-ness? That is a quandary that's been debated since the beginning of human beings.

Life is what it is. If you venture into the world, there are those ready to attack—especially if you are or are doing something special. I absolutely hate that this is a truth of life. But that truth doesn't care if you and I hate it—we still have to face it.

Venture into the ocean, and you might become victim to a shark who is hungry or feeling threatened by your presence or is just doing what it is genetically programmed to do: attack and consume. The shark may take a bite out of you and remove a limb or reveal your innards, and then swim off, not thinking a thing about it. However, the smell of blood brings other

*I*f there are any marks at all
of special design in creation,
one of the things most evidently
designed is that a large
proportion of all animals should
pass their existence in
tormenting and devouring
other animals.

—John Stuart Mill

sharks to feed in a frenzy of excitement—leaving nothing of you other than the memories of you cherished by your loved ones.

Sharks have no remorse, no morality, no sense of fairness, no concern about the consequences of their actions—as long as their instinctive needs are satisfied.

I find that there are a lot of human beings who are just like that—hence the title of this book.

So, then, what do we do to survive shark attacks . . . on land?

Read on.

DR. LAURA SCHLESSINGER

2010

Chapter One

The Nature of Betrayal

There are two types of people in this world: good and bad. The good sleep better, but the bad seem to enjoy the waking hours much more.

—Woody Allen

No matter what type of person you are, there are really bad people out there who are ready to disrupt your world and well-being to a magnitude you never imagined. If you don't know or believe that, you are dangerously naive. If you believe that all the people out there are bad, you are dangerously paranoid. In between those two extremes is the truth of the sad nature of human beings with which we must all contend: betrayals are commonplace.

Betrayals are a breach of trust to a code or a person, including acts of dishonesty, lying, cheating, or stealing, double-crossing, deception, gossiping, duplicity, unfaithfulness, treason, leading astray, undermining, selling out . . . to name only a few faces of betrayal.

Every single human being on the face of the earth has been betrayed, back-stabbed, undermined, screwed over, or had their reputation attacked at least once in their lives. It's a horrible experience, leaving you stunned, scared, sad, and very, very angry; and sometimes you become so cynical that it changes fundamental ways you think and react to people for a long, long time.

Some folks so assaulted end up abusing drugs and alcohol, recede into the background of life with depression, or adopt a "scorched earth" mentality of being angry with everybody and everything because of their pain and inability to get apologies or compensations or any relief whatsoever.

When you are attacked, the first reaction is shock and disbelief. Next you try to shut down what is happening. When that doesn't work, you strike back—which usually makes the situation worse. After a while you turn to others for solace, emotional support, and assistance in getting the betrayer to back off.

You probably found that most people were sympathetic at first, and then they didn't want to hear about it anymore. You also probably found that not too many people would step up to the plate and speak up for you. Why? Because they don't want a bull's-eye pasted onto their backs next. People who betray are very powerful because "good people" are more than willing to stand by and do nothing to avoid discomfort in their own lives.

The darkest places in hell are reserved for those who maintain their neutrality in times of moral crisis.

—Dante Alighieri

That means that adding insult (no valiant supporters rushing to your side) to injury (the betrayal) becomes your personal reality. Expecting rallying support from people becomes a huge disappointment added on to the original betrayal. In fact, the whole battalion taking a step back when you ask for volunteers to help you fight your battle can be a more devastating experience than the original betrayal. You end up being not only victimized but abandoned to fight your fight alone. It makes you wonder what friends are for. It makes you also doubt the legal and social systems that appear to lean way over backward to protect the perps.

I keep forgetting that being "Dr. Laura," while it may be a blessing in that I am able to help people be and do better in their lives, brings with it certain problems stemming from the perceptions, envy, resentment, or competitiveness of others. I naively keep thinking I can easily be "one of the guys," when that is just not the case. This hope gets me in trouble. I was recently invited to be on the board of a nonprofit organization involved in an activity dear to my heart. I thought, Maybe this time I can be "one of the guys" and use my celebrity to help them do some great public service activities. The head of this organization and one of the more important members were very enthusiastic . . . and so I was swept along with my good intentions ready and willing.

I went to the first board meeting, and three members were waiting outside in the cold and dark for someone to open the locked door. When we couldn't find the persons with the keys, I suggested with all the warmth and enthusiasm in my heart, "Next time, why don't we have the meeting in my home?" I thought that would make it more comfortable and homey.

One of the three turned on me with quite a pinched face and said—brace yourself—"Don't think you can come here and throw your weight around."

My jaw dropped—I thought I'd entered the Twilight Zone. I countered gently with, "I'm not trying to throw weight around. I just offered my home." He repeated himself twice. I woke up and smelled the sewer. I said, "OK, then," and turned and walked away, realizing that for some people, their little world is their place of power and perceived importance; my ability to help them, while it might seem like a plus for many, would be a personal demotion in the minds of some.

Now for the betrayal. One of the three waiting in the dark was a "friend" who stood quietly—didn't say a word. He could have said, "Hey, she's just trying to be helpful. . . . it's okay . . . calm it down." I don't know . . . something!

He could have called me later that night or the next day to commiserate. Something!

That the first guy was a jerk is simply annoying, like a mosquito. That my "friend" stood by . . . that's the part that hurts and made me sad.

The next day, the man in charge who'd invited me in the first place offered his apologies for the egregious behavior of that member, and said also that I should reconsider withdrawing from the board. He offered that there were asses in every group of people.

I thought about that for an hour, and wrote back that the only reason all groups of people have asses is that the decent people keep them around.

No answer back to that.

The "stand by" folks try to defend their inaction by first minimizing the betrayal. They might tell you it's really a small issue, it's not important enough for you to bother with, most people don't even pay attention to him/her anyway, it will blow over, just ignore it/him/ her, try to go make nice-nice or, the best old standby, "You be the bigger person."

Now, there just might be circumstances where it is true that this really isn't a biggie. In which case, a good night's sleep after a glass of medicinal wine might just be what the shrink ordered. Perhaps this is only a misunderstanding that can be easily rectified with a friendly conversation aimed at clarification and a reestablishment of bonds.

And now for the big "however." . . . You are usually wise enough—especially after a night of sleeping on it—to know the difference between a glitch in communication and a frank betrayal of your trust, faith, privacy, truth, status, reputation, relationships, and so forth.

Do betrayers mean to be bad? Ultimately, given the havoc they wreak and the pain and emotional devastation they cause . . . it really doesn't matter. I do believe strongly that people who do bad things range from sociopathic personalities to the everyday individual who justifies his or her bad behavior in the most extraordinary ways. It is not the sociopath that should worry you the most. It is the everyday people, in service to their own egos, social status, financial opportunities, envy, and petty meanness, you have to worry about the most, as they are likely to pop up from the most unlikely places: school, church, family, neighborhood, circle of friends, work . . . anywhere you interact with people.

Do these people know that they are "bad" or have done something "bad"? I talk to people every day who have performed the most egregious acts of hurt and betrayal, yet deny that their behaviors weren't righteous. Righteous! They try to give examples of what was done to them (usually innocuous) and convince me that their actions were necessary or justified. These "everyday" folks often just don't think about the humanity of their victims at all, and in fact would deny that their targets even are victims.

It comes down to this: hurting other people feels good when it is in the service of the hurter's ego. Plain and simple. It is an endorphin and adrenaline rush to have godlike power over the life of another human being who has or is something you want or wish to be.

When someone tries to explain to these people that what they are doing is wrong, obsessive, vicious, or evil, they will not back down. To back down by admitting to wrongdoing would be such an assault on their inner well-being that it is to be avoided at all costs. They will argue forever that they are justified, even if it means making up facts or distorting partial truths. Fighting off the attempts of even their friends to get them to stop what they are doing, they will likely bring up delusional-sounding rationalizations such as that they have somehow been influenced by their target. Blaming the target for any and all discontent or disagreement or criticism of their actions just further fans their flames of justification.

Ultimately, they can't give up their self-perceived righteous position, because to admit they were wrong—no, admit they *did* wrong—is a concept that completely overwhelms them. Their inner sense is that it would ultimately make them look deceitful, mean, obsessed, petty, venomous, stupid, and bad. Obviously, those possibilities are to be avoided at all costs. Betrayers rarely give in or give up. That's another factor that makes them so fundamentally scary.

Every now and then—as I have experienced on the air with callers—people who have betrayed others will struggle with me but eventually admit that they simply needed to change the way the world was looking to them and how they perceived how they looked in that world by destroying, damaging, or hurting someone else, to take the critical gaze from within and without off them.

In other words—though I don't want to evoke sympathy for betrayers—some folks out to get others and probably hurting inside themselves decide on betrayal to make other people feel their pain; they make themselves feel better by causing pain rather than just feeling it. Why no sympathy? Because there are other ways to deal with individual pain, frustration, and disappointment; not the least of which is simply getting spiritual or psychological help. We have free will—and the fundamentals of character demand that we deal with our hurt, confusion, and existential anger in ways that cause no pain to others. Nonetheless, there is always collateral damage. It is when that damage is planned that we start to see the snake seducing Eve.

I recently spoke on air to a woman with two children, one four and the other eighteen months, who had finally left a physically abusive marriage. She said her culture, her parents, and her minister all conspired to have her stay in this dangerous situation. Now that she was out, she was so enraged with her husband for hurting and destroying her life, family, and dreams that she found herself turning it on her little four-year-old son. She knew she shouldn't, but she "just couldn't help" herself. Nonsense. She is just like her husband: feeling small, stupid, and disappointed with life and turning on somebody weaker to feel better about herself.

She had the power to make the decision not to have babies with such an immature and dangerous man; her son has no such power, and is a virtual prisoner of her unwillingness to admit to her own weakness. Her husband projected his weakness on her and punished it outside of himself, and she is starting to do the same thing. They have both betrayed the person they are supposed to love and protect.

I worked hard to explain this to her. When it was clear I wasn't getting through—and I was worried about the well-being of her son—I told her that for the same reason she left her abusive husband, her child should leave her . . . but can't. She seemed absolutely stunned—which was my intent. I often have to shock callers into a realization of what they don't want to know: that the enemy is now themselves.

I gave her alternatives to destroying her flesh and blood because of her shame at being with and tolerating such a man, and at caving under the nonsensical pressure of those around her who betrayed her by pressuring her to "keep a marriage and family together" no matter what. I suggested that she contact CPS (child protective services), that she give primary responsibility of the children to her mother, and that she seek psychological help to accept her own nature and improve it. I reminded her that she had the strength and the good sense to finally get out of a bad situation—with no support—and that now she ought to use that courage and wisdom to help herself.

There are two ways to become "more." One is to fuel your own flame (which this mother did by leaving her abusive husband) and make it brighter; the other is to dim or eliminate the light of others (which she was starting to do with her small son). Unfortunately, destruction seems to be easier to accomplish; it takes little time, planning, or effort. Simply by contrast, then, you seem the brighter light. Flames burn in hell too . . . but I wouldn't call that an improvement on the dark.

There are a significant number of motivations behind the actions of betrayers. They are in totality too many to list and explain, so I will select the most typical. You will no doubt recognize these descriptions as fitting people you have known, and maybe have been . . . or are.

Let's start with the basics: there are things that are simply right to do, and there are things that are wrong to do. While people may argue the rightness and wrongness of any particular issue, my best way of making someone admit to something's wrongness is to have them imagine that thing done to them. Suddenly then it all becomes clear. There actually were people arguing in print in the mainstream press that it was wrong for the brother of the Unabomber to have turned his brother in because he betrayed "blood." While that is very Mafia-like in its romanticizing of so-called family loyalty, the brother did not betray what was right: protecting the lives of others by having his murderous brother apprehended. Blood should never be thicker than morality.

I bet if the naysayers knew that the next target of the Unabomber was themselves or their children, they would suddenly "get" that values and ideals are more important to the quality of humanity than DNA or blood oaths.

The Unabomber's brother is not, in my mind, an example of a betrayer, as some proclaimed. He is an example of an exceptionally moral and compassionate man who plainly valued truth and the sanctity of life. He is a hero, not a betrayer.

Now to true betrayers—and while they apparently vary so much in motivation, truly it comes down to one main factor: life should be all about "me"; what makes me happy, what makes me look good, what gets me what I want, what besides me explains my failures, how I can make others hurt like I hurt, how I can take from others what ought to be mine, how I can seem more important and powerful. It is all about the "me." And the universal "you" just becomes a mean to the end: "me."

POSSESSIVENESS

Imagine making new friends, only to find them getting ever more cold and distant. For the life of you, you can't imagine what has happened, and it's uncomfortable to try to get information out of them. Then imagine discovering that one of your prior friends has been poisoning their minds about you to turn them away from you. Imagine going to that original friend and presenting point-blank the proof that they've been spreading horrendous lies about you, your marriage, your children, your mothering, and so forth. Why would a "friend" do that? The answer is a horrible distortion of biblical writings: "There shall be no friends before me."

The so-called friend's betrayal of the friendship by spreading disgusting gossip about my caller was not meant to directly hurt her at all, but rather to eliminate all competition so that the "friend" couldn't possibly lose the friendship. Clearly, she believed that she was only going to be seen as a valued friend if there were no one else to compare with—and some people see sharing as minimizing their gains. Possessiveness comes from insecurity. I always tell those who are insecure that the best way to become secure in a relationship is by becoming the kind of person they themselves would always love to have in their lives. Of course, the mere idea of needing self-improvement bruises the ego, which is frail to start out with, so defensiveness becomes the main obstacle, and gossip and its destruction are just darn easier.

This possessiveness—a dislike of your spending time with other friends or family or at school or other outside activities because they will help you see him as he sees himself (as lacking), and thus cause you to leave him—is one of the first warning signs that a friend or spouse is potentially dangerous. The frightening betrayal of vows to "love, honor, cherish" by threats or actual violence comes from a fear of not being lovable. Talk about a self-fulfilling prophesy!

The focus of possessive people is not on the relationship at all. The focus is only on their fears and needs. These people are perpetually insensitive to the needs and feelings of others. These are difficult people to please and satisfy. And if they feel you haven't sufficiently pleased or satisfied them, they will betray you as they believe you have betrayed them by having other friends, or just having a life (children, hobbies, work, travel).

ENTITLEMENT

There is often a problem with two roles being intertwined. For example: doing business with family or friends, or becoming friends with people you do business with. Because of the "friend" status, people start to feel a sense of entitlement, as if they should have special compensations and treatment. They believe that the normal rules and expectations in a work situation do not apply to them. This makes some people get very demanding. When people develop these unreasonable expectations, and these expectations are not met—because they are anywhere from not fair to outrageous—they usually get angry. The Internet has become a marvelous way to hurt others at little expense, and often with complete anonymity. Friendships and business relationships and common decency are suspended as the "entitled" individual wreaks havoc on the other's life, often posting disgusting accusations that can never be taken back or properly remedied once dispersed in cyberspace.

Interestingly and ironically, it is the wrongdoers who feel "betrayed," when in truth, nobody did anything to them—they decided unilaterally on unreasonable game rules, and rebelled when these rules magically didn't apply. They are the betrayers of the friendship, work relationship, and values of fair play.

COMPETITION

It is probably the oldest story there is: remember the wonderful movie, *All About Eve*? Well, an aspiring actress kisses up to a star, the ultimate goal being to take the star's career, friends, and fiancé. This sort of scenario is so typical in organizations such as charity groups, work situations, church committees, community task forces, politics, hierarchies in law enforcement, military—wherever there are people, there will be sibling rivalry for attention from superiors as there was for attention from parents, and ambitious people will try to eliminate those who they perceive as getting in the way of their progress simply by existing, much less being competent.

Backstabbing at work or in those committees is standard. I don't know anyone who has worked in a group who hasn't complained that someone went behind his back to complain about something or other he was supposed to have said or done—all to advance the complainer's own position in the organization. Frighteningly, this is also true of religious groups. Of the more than one thousand e-mails I got commenting on the subject matter of this book, an inordinately high number were complaining about situations regarding their church! You'd think that people who are in a religious community would walk the prayers, but people tend to be people no matter where they are—considerations of God or charity do not deflect the individual who wishes to be on the top of that heap.

Backstabbing is quite effective when executed with precision. All someone has to do is plant poisonous seeds with the right people—people gossip—and down goes your reputation before you even know what didn't hit you directly. People will definitely lie intentionally to get your job or position, and not even blink. When and if they get caught, and when and if there are any consequences, they will just move on and repeat their pattern because they see the world and its inhabitants as walls to blast through or people to walk over: dog eat dog—and if you can't hack it, too bad. They see life as war and feel totally justified in fighting for their desired position, so they have no remorse whatsoever.

DEFENSIVENESS

In my life and on my radio program I stand up for certain principles, two of which are: that voluntary day care is child neglect, and that we should make an effort to be fit by moving more and eating less. I probably get the most pointed and personal criticisms and attacks because I discuss how people ought to lead their lives. I give my opinions; people are free to take them or leave them. I am, of course, trying to influence people in a way that I believe will directly make their lives more fulfilling and happier. However, the road to that destination requires embracing certain values, making sacrifices, and living for something and someone outside of oneself.

When some folks listen to me and perceive a chasm between my ideals and their lifestyle choices (abortion versus adoption, day care versus raising one's own children, marriage versus shacking up, no dating when divorced with minor children, marital lovemaking versus hooking up, children are best served by a mommy and a daddy—married, and so forth), they get very uncomfortable, and often they want to shoot the messenger. Hence, some of the most vicious Web sites, often almost totally dedicated to smearing me, fill the Internet.

I can tell you about two cases in which I knew in advance that the individuals involved would likely betray journalistic integrity to deal with their own defensiveness about my positions versus their lifestyle. They were both doing pieces about me for national magazines. I found out that one had all her children in day care, and the other, a quite overweight journalist, commented, while eating a highly caloric chicken salad sandwich with lotsa mayo, about how tiny I was as I had a turkey on rye with lettuce and tomato. In both cases I knew I was toast . . . and I was right.

The "lotsa mayo" journalist was a real pip. She'd been friends for twenty years with my then chief of staff. She called my staffer and—well—lied about what she wanted to do. She said I was a sociological phenomenon, and she wanted to do a piece for *Vanity Fair* exploring said phenomenon. My then editor from HarperCollins warned me not to do it—again and again and again. She pleaded with me. What she didn't do was tell me she had a friend at the magazine who was at the planning meeting for this article on me, and it was set up to be an attack (she told me years later—gee, thanks—guess she didn't want to hurt her friendship with the informant).

Well, stupid me, I went with the advice of my staffer, and sure enough, it didn't take long to discover that the journalist was just accumulating nasty comments from envious competitors, twisting truths, omitting truths that were positive, and so forth. The article was utterly disgusting and hurtful.

Yet I still remember the first day she sat with me to watch me do my show, and she, obese, ate the ultra-mayo chicken salad sandwich, sneering down at my body as I went to sit at the microphone, declaring, "What are you? A size zero?" As I said, I knew right then and there that I was in trouble.

Wow. The levels of betrayal. This journalist lied to her friend of twenty years and to me. My editor/publisher withheld crucial information that would have protected me because she didn't want to betray her friend, who was betraying his company by telling her the information. And various people, all women, contributed ugly "information" because, frankly, I was successful and they weren't.

Amusingly, one of the complaints all these unsuccessful competitors had is that I don't get along with women. Most of my "peeps" are women—they are unaware of such issues—haha.

Those who contributed to producing this attack piece of me had their fifteen minutes of feeling important and powerful. Then they went back to their lives, and I continued to work hard and maintain my dignity.

Introspection and correction are more difficult than attacking, and many people who recognize the distinction between what they are doing and what they probably ought to be doing often feel guilt that turns into defensiveness, which often turns into lashing out by betrayal.

As one listener wrote, "She [referring to her wicked sister-in-law] has never liked us because we are the voice of reason." Evidently, the listener's husband was considered too judgmental because he told his sister that at twenty-eight she ought not to keep letting Mom and Dad support her, and she should spend more than

*The universe seems bankrupt
as soon as we begin to discuss
the characters of individuals.*

—Henry David Thoreau

three months getting to know a guy she met on the Internet before they married. Oops. There goes that nasty good sense.

The sister-in-law intentionally planned and threw herself a wedding party on the day the listener's baby— prediagnosed with a heart anomaly that would probably be terminal—was to be born. The family further betrayed their own son and his wife and ill grandchild by not showing up at the hospital and going to the party instead because they were "afraid" of the ruckus she would put up if they didn't, regardless of the emotional cost to these grieving parents.

This is yet another case of supposedly good people standing by and letting the self-centered brat continue her antics because they are afraid of her. Afraid of what? That she'll yell and scream and call names? Two words: *so* and *what.* For an aggressive brat, they all betrayed their "good" family members in profound need and their own values.

GREED

There is one darkly hilarious scene in *Zorba the Greek* in which the old lady is dying, and all her relatives are around the bed . . . waiting. She seems to sigh her last, and the relatives start grabbing furnishings and any other objects of value. Then the old lady seems to revive, and they drop everything and feign concern once again. This goes back and forth a few times until she finally dies. While it is humorous to watch in the movie, this is less funny in real life. Not only do family members bite and scratch each other, try to influence the dying to give them a disproportionate amount of the upcoming estate, but siblings and other relatives will lie, cheat, and steal—simply for money and things. And these are people who don't perceive themselves as greedy! They rationalize that they are somehow entitled because of their need, because of some imagined slight that the parental money would make up for, or because they are jealous of the quality lives of others who stand to inherit. Ooh, it can get ugly, and families are often totally destroyed by these situations, where money becomes a substitute for love, importance, or retribution.

Sibling will betray sibling, other family members will collude or have their own campaign, ersatz religious organizations might manipulate the goodwill of the soon-to-be-departed—as well as their fears of death and an afterlife.

But life-and-death situations are not the only settings for greed-driven betrayal. There are folks who buy property or businesses together, who purchase lottery tickets together, who invest together, and when the windfall does come in, decide that the agreements and promises shouldn't hold true because of . . . something petty, untrue, unfair, unreasonable, and not moral. Doesn't matter, though—money is often thicker than morals, values, promises, and friendships.

JEALOUSY

People will try to ruin the happiness of others they perceive as being as happy as they'd like to be. They try to steal each other's love objects, interfere with their attempts to lose weight or other avenues of personal betterment, give them bad advice in the hopes that the others lose what they wish to have, turn others against them because they wish they were them, and on and on.

Jealousy and envy are biblical breaches. The final commandments of the Ten have to do with not coveting thy neighbor's anything. Coveting leads to ignoring the blessings you do have, turns your heart and mind against others simply because of their efforts and good fortune—bringing out the worst in you—and certainly does not motivate you to better yourself. It only motivates you to steal and destroy.

Competitiveness is in and of itself a good thing—if it brings out your best efforts. But it becomes something quite frightening if it brings out the impulse to destroy anything that makes you see yourself wanting.

The types who work to destroy the happiness and well-being of others they envy are particularly dangerous, as they generally intend directly to do harm. Hence, we have athletes who try to break the knees of Olympic ice-skaters who might beat them for the gold, mothers who actually kill somebody else's children to make sure their own child gets on the cheerleading squad (both true stories!), a teen lover who pours acid on the face of her adult boyfriend's wife, and parents who will kill or maim or kidnap their own child to hurt the spouse who left them.

In every case, people betray their own values, good sense, responsibility to others, rules, fairness, laws, moral values, and common decency to get something they want.

UNHAPPINESS

"I'm not happy" is the stated reason for spouses defending their decision to break their marital vows. And unhappiness is often at the center of the decision to breach the sanctity of the marriage. It is, however, a decision, chosen from one of many alternatives. Betraying vows taken in public and shared by friends and family and God is a major step, and people need to take responsibility for having made that choice. Contrary to what many try to convince others, things do not "just happen." Invitations and temptations are always present in everyone's life. How we respond to them is the measure of our character and commitment to someone else as well as our own conscience.

Now it is true that if you're neglected or abused in your marriage, you will be more likely to find solace in the arms of another. However, this is an abuse of the "other," as well as an action that threatens the very structure of your immediate and extended family. It could go even further than that if you are a clergy member or politician whose honesty is trusted as a part of your functions.

While you may be justified in your unhappiness within the marriage, a revealed betrayal of vows of fidelity erodes trust that others have in you in all other aspects of your relationships and responsibilities. It is a public—not just a private—betrayal.

IDENTITY

There are some people who derive the major part of their identity by betraying all rules of social appropriateness. They will lie, mislead, undermine, backstab, gossip, and attempt to isolate and alienate somebody in particular. Why? Because when they attack somebody, hate that person with a passion, and are committed to hurting him, they feel a sense of importance and power. They usually justify their actions based on some generally minor issue—a difference in politics, a disappointment, or a fear of losing (or the pain of having lost) some position of significance.

These are generally people whose lives are not full in the sense of rich and deep. Anything that in their own minds—but not necessarily in reality—threatens their tenuous position in the scheme of their lives is met by viciousness. Most try to be anonymous, but some love to be right out there with it. Their brazenness comes from the belief that the reason they don't get criticized about their actions is that all agree with them—when in fact, some people are afraid of them or benefit from them in some other way they don't wish to undermine, and others just don't care about things that don't impact them directly.

EVIL

I remember all the attempts to analyze the Hillside Stranglers in Los Angeles a few decades ago. The reason we always try to make sense of horrors is that we figure if we understand it, then we can control it. So all sorts of pop-psych types came out of the mist to analyze the motivations of men who would torture, rape, sodomize, and kill other human beings as though it were a hobby. Lots of potential diagnoses were tossed about—and of course, defense attorneys often turn to mental illness or temporary insanity pleas if it really looks bad for the perp.

I was relieved to see a documentary wherein a psychiatrist said quite clearly, "There is evil." She did not mean demonic possession. She meant that there are people for whom doing evil deeds is plainly their norm. They are entertained and pleased by these acts. Think of the Joker in the Batman movie *Dark Knight*, who simply lived to wreak havoc and chaos and show the power of evil and the weakness of good. This was his purpose, and he enjoyed it to the end—and, frankly, was quite good at it.

There is no understanding evil. But there is a huge necessity for identifying it as it is and not trying to dismiss or minimize it, which just provides the evildoer with more opportunities and victims with less defenses.

EXPEDIENCE

To my mind, this is the most egregious, most devastating form of betrayal—worse even than evil—because it is the most cold, most thought-out, most intentional. To know that someone turned on you simply—and I mean that word, *simply*—because it served them at that moment in time to be a turncoat, to betray your confidences and friendship, is devastating. It makes you feel as though you basically don't matter—and you're right, you don't.

Expedient betrayals are the most personal, and probably hurt the most too; you are forced to realize that all you did and were and are for that person just didn't matter at all in the end. All that matters for people like this is getting in the right place with the right people at the right time to take care of themselves. Sorry! You are but a small inconvenience in the way of attaining an advantage in some way in any organization or group of people.

The ultimate pain of betrayals, greater than the havoc and misfortune and embarrassment they cause, is the feeling they give you of helplessness, irrationality, and hopelessness, and the obvious awareness that you as a human being could be so easily dispensed with, as though you had no importance whatsoever. That hurts; that hurts deeply.

REVENGE

When people are betrayed, they learn that they are capable of emotions they never wanted to have: hate, rage, and the profound need to get revenge. That level of anger is a powerful emotion that causes you to inflict great pain and devastation on your betrayer. It can make you feel quite obsessed and ill, disrupt your entire life and all your other relationships—in spite of how wonderful they might be—and even get you to the point of feeling like you're going to lose your mind to the one idea: revenge.

You may think about revenge every day. You may beat yourself up, thinking you've been so good to the betrayer, you don't deserve this, you are helpless, your life is lost, you can never be happy again.

Truthfully, there isn't always a happy ending. Justice is rarely met. Revenge can bite you back in your butt. Good doesn't always prevail. Bad and evil seem to persist.

So now what?

Keep reading.

Chapter Two

Betrayal or Not a Betrayal . . . That Is the Question

Misery is almost always the result of thinking.

—Joseph Joubert

Now that I've made some of you nervously hyperalert to betrayals from just about anywhere, it is important for us to be able to honestly weed out true betrayals from things that look like betrayals, feel like betrayals, sound like betrayals—but aren't betrayals at all.

Recently, a young mother called, just beside herself that her mother would betray her confidence and talk badly behind her back. Whew! Of course that sounded serious! I asked her to elaborate. It seems that her mother wrote an e-mail complaining about my caller to the caller's sister, but accidently sent the e-mail to my caller. Ouch; so far sounds like a kind of betrayal.

I asked about the content of the e-mail. Basically, the mother was complaining to the sister that both of them did a lot for my caller, helping her with the kids, babysitting, and so forth, but that the caller had been offended because neither of them was willing to babysit for her the weekend before. The mother went on to say that they (mother and daughter) had their own lives, and had done a lot for her (my caller), and that her response to this one situation was upsetting.

I told the caller that my interpretation of the e-mail was quite different from hers. All she saw was the complaining about her between her sister and her mother. I saw the mother and sister sharing a feeling that she was not all that grateful and gracious for what they did do for her, since she reacted so badly the one time they wouldn't or couldn't.

Furthermore, reading this e-mail gave her a heads-up on her behavior; she needed to feel less entitled and more appreciative. I suggested she tell both her mom and sister that she had read this e-mail and was humbled and apologetic; all would be forgiven, and she would have learned an important lesson in how to give and take in relationships instead of seeing herself as the sole member of the universe.

She became angry with me. I told her that if she assumed the appropriate responsibility in this affair, it could be made "all better" in minutes. If she was going to dig her heels in and declare betrayal simply because a discussion was going on behind her back that didn't make her seem so special, all bets were going to be off, and she'd be on her own—angry.

Sometimes it takes time for people I speak to on my radio program to drop their defensiveness and ego and wrap themselves around the uncomfortable truth. She was one of those people. Nonetheless, the listening audience learns something valuable from each caller, whether or not the caller joins them in that lesson at that very moment in time.

Learning lessons is an important part of life. One listener described a youth of feeling like a number of friends were specifically out to get her, each for their own reasons. They may have said what she found to be hurtful things that rattled her inner being, and felt like daggers stabbing into her heart. She found herself feeling and behaving like a pathetic victim, paralyzed with self-pity.

She, perceiving herself as helplessly demeaned, did not even consider revenge on these friends; rather, she turned the revenge inward, walking away, allowing herself to feel empty and alone. This went on for many years until, with maturity, she realized these friends were not out to hurt her by betraying the imagined rule of friendship: Do no harm. The hurt came from truths that she wasn't ready to accept; they were simply trying to point out painful realities about her selfish and immature behavior in an attempt to help her grow. In hindsight, most of the time she was at least partly to blame, and too self-centered to admit it.

She has moved past the perception that these friends were betraying her affections, to a place where she feels actually thankful for all of those friendships, including perhaps the ones who didn't quite have the best intentions. After all, they are all the people who have shaped her and given her higher standards. She can use these circumstances to reflect on how she can be a better friend and set a loving example that kindness and love are what ultimately matter the most—or she can continue to feel martyred on the altar of betrayed friendships.

In other words, when she opened her mind and heart to the truths of their "hurtful" words, it helped her to be a better person and friend. To allow her to accept what is fulfilling and empowering.

This latter story clarifies the difference between feeling hurt and actually being hurt by someone's intent to hurt. This seems to be a stumbling block of misunderstanding for so many. One of my favorite examples of this is the true-life story shared by a lot of people: ignoring reality and then being hurt and angry—and

vengeful—that fantasies didn't magically turn into realities because you wanted them to.

One caller told me about her involvement in an on-
again, off-again relationship with a man. Every time
they got back together, it was because she thought he
had changed and he thought she had changed—but
no one had changed. The corker was recently catch-
ing him with another woman, which, of course, he lied
about—no kidding. She called me because, as she said,
"I am consumed with this incredible urge for revenge."

I came back with, "You should be consumed with
a sense of total abject stupidity." I went on to explain
that one of the aspects of revenge that most interests
me is how people go there to blame the other person
for their own stupidity. The minute people tell me the
"on-again, off-again" story, I can see that they volun-
teered for nonsense, and nonsense is what they got.

I explained that he didn't betray her; he stayed true
to his nature. If it's an elephant, you give it peanuts,
you don't give it yogurt and then complain it won't
eat. When you choose unwisely and keep going back
into an untenable situation, it is your own damn fault;
you can't blame the other person. Getting revenge in
those circumstances is continued stupidity, because it
presumes that the other party is responsible; and he's
not— you are!

When the caller wanted to know what she should do with the intense feelings of revenge that were overpowering her, I suggested she say to herself, "I am one silly lady to have been fooling around with a guy like this for so long. I have to look inside myself to see what I was trying to prove or avoid and improve myself. I have to learn from this."

It's quite humbling to move from righteous vengeance to personal insight. Vengeance won't get you where you want and need to go in this circumstance; introspection will.

It is disconcerting, at the least, to accept that you actually set up your own betrayal—but that happens every day. It is surprising to hear from so many women in particular who put themselves in obviously no-win situations and then complain about being betrayed by the other person. One woman wrote me that she'd been involved for four years with a man who is twenty-five years older than she, continues to be separated from his spouse, and has a seventeen-year-old child. Amazingly, she didn't find out these particulars until after the first year of their relationship—now that was a betrayal! He engaged her in a relationship under false pretenses—that he was available. It was at this point that she should have

Don't sweat the petty things and don't pet the sweaty things.

—George Carlin

bailed out and told him off as a self-centered, deceitful betrayer of affection.

But she didn't. Sob. She stayed around for three more years of hearing about his impending divorce and marriage to her. For those three years, she betrayed herself. Her anger at him is no longer valid. Any notions of revenge are a deceit on her part, as she made the choice to play the game out for three more years.

She wrote that her revenge will be to allow him to come to her college graduation, then announce that she will not marry him and move on with her life.

Yeah, I'm sure that'll really teach him. Self-deluding to the end. Leaving this unfortunate situation is a good idea; I wish she were doing it for the right reason (good sense) and not for the wrong reason (imagined revenge).

It is, as I said, not unusual for people to set themselves up for disappointment and imagined betrayal, and then be angry with the wrong person. I love romantic endings, but not those that include a lack of good common sense. Women call me all the time to inquire whether they should drop their lives to go chase some guy, sacrifice everything they have (home, job, school, friends) to be with some guy they just know is the love of their lives. Perhaps they reconnected years after high school, or met on the Internet—whatever the circumstances, they allow themselves to act quite irrationally in order to have the romantic dream.

One woman wrote to me that within three months of being reunited with a high-school boyfriend, she made the decision on her own to withdraw from her graduate school program, put in her notice to quit her job, and give up her apartment. This was not done, by the way, with some mutual plan to immediately marry. She did this to increase her chances, she thought, of having him be her man.

By the time she arrived in his state, he didn't want to have contact. When she tracked him down, he said that he had changed his mind, that he didn't want her to move there to be with him, and that he wasn't in love with her like he'd thought he was.

I constantly tell women that chasing a man is unappealing to him. What a man doesn't have to work toward or fight for, he generally doesn't respect or value.

These are examples of setting yourself up in an unrealistic way, and then proclaiming betrayal when fantasies do not morph into reality.

Setting yourself up can also assume the form of bad deeds coming back to bite you. One caller to my radio program complained to me that she used to gossip with a coworker about various people and things that went on around the office. Well, after a while, the caller discovered that this coworker was absorbing and recycling gossip from others about her, and before she knew it, there were repercussions with a supervisor about the stories being told about her at work.

Well, isn't that a tough way to learn the lesson that gossip is never harmless! Do not gossip with people. If they'll do it with you, they'll do it to you too!

Let me repeat that: if they'll do it *with* you, they'll do it *to* you. This is the ugly part of what-goes-around-comes-around.

Sometimes, though, people get upset and feel betrayed by things that truly have nothing to do with them—not really. For example, imagine that you are part of a group of people working on some community, charitable, or social project, and some of the people start disagreeing with how and when to do certain things. Let's imagine for a moment that the people arguing are your parents and some other couple. Let's add that there is nobody doing anything wrong—just an honest disagreement—but feelings are getting roused anyway.

This is the scenario one listener wrote in with. She considered the other couple as betrayers of her because, "If they were truly my friends, they wouldn't have attacked my parents so." Her thinking was that they would calculate her feelings into all their decisions. In reality, we each have to learn that we have to remove our tender feelings each time somebody else has feelings to the contrary of what we'd hoped. They are allowed to feel how they do, just as you are allowed your own set of feelings. It doesn't mean one is right or wrong, just different.

And you can't use loyalty as a weapon to make sure others feel the way you wish they would. That's just not fair. What is fair is to be up front immediately when you "feel hurt." People tend to avoid communication that might clarify and mediate a situation; instead they grow in anger and resentment, marinating in their own perspective on circumstances. That's obviously not a good trade-off for the temporary discomfort of having an honest, open discussion, showing great compassion for the fact that others see things through the prism of their own experiences and desires. It isn't necessarily about you at all!

Deciding to take a boat out in the perfect storm is just not wise, and clearly potentially suicidal. The crew may decide that it's worth the risk of death to get a great catch of fish and make a financial killing; sadly, however, the killing typically turns out to be directed toward the risk-takers.

I see the same thing happening time after time: people assume an obviously low-percentage good-outcome risk will turn out well, and then when it goes the way any observer would guess, get angry and vengeful.

One typical scenario in this category is marrying into a situation with a dangerous and destructive ex-intimate and minor children, even after being warned. For years, as one caller described it, she was under attack from her husband's ex-girlfriend, with whom he shared a daughter. They married when the child was two, after he had warned her about the ex-girlfriend and how dangerously vicious she was. My caller blithely believed that love conquered all, and she could deal with anything, and married anyway.

The ex-girlfriend accused her of performing oral sex in front of the daughter, of losing her in shopping centers, of physically abusing the children that my caller had with her husband. Police were called, as were child protective services, and reports were made to the caller's church to inform the pastor that his sweet Sunday school teacher was really a horrible and evil person.

When behavior is expected, it is no longer a betrayal. This woman was threatened with the loss of her own children, and her anger and fear started to show in her attitude toward her stepdaughter, since the little girl was a potential threat. If the little girl told her mother anything that could be construed negatively, my caller could end up in prison. This obviously hurt the marriage also.

They eventually sent the daughter to live with the mother to avoid the threat to their own family. It is amazing that vicious, jealous people like this ex-girlfriend cannot be touched by the law or child protective services, but generally are free to go on and on with their venomous attacks.

Coexisting with this kind of fear is not good for living creatures. I don't recommend that we volunteer for situations like this, with our good intentions and wishful thinking, when there is so much damage that can be done to all the participants—except the evildoer, of course. But certainly, if you put yourself in this position, you put a bull's-eye on your own behind as well as those of others—and for that, you have to assume responsibility. Certainly, while you might be being victimized, you signed up for the adventure.

Basically, if you get in bed with dogs, you can expect to catch fleas, ticks, and dirty hairs. One listener wrote that she went through a horrible ordeal that ended up in her completely disowning her father, with whom she "thinks" she had always been close. He had always exhibited sociopathic behavior; both her grandfather and her two ex-stepmothers told her that he had been diagnosed as sociopathic. When he reached the age of fifty, he began to do even more questionable things, some of which he wanted her to lie to the authorities about in order to protect him.

When her father helped her teenage brother and his girlfriend cross the state line because the girlfriend's parents wouldn't allow her to date the brother, they were caught, and her father was charged with kidnapping, among other things. When my listener went to court to testify, she told the truth about what she knew. That's when he turned on her.

Look, friends, when somebody does bad things and you stand by them because you feel special being the only one close to, for example, "Daddy," realize that you are cuddling up next to a venomous cobra. As long as you are keeping it warm, it may not strike. The moment you stop giving the cobra what it wants—you are toast.

This caller complained that her father had ripped the rug out from under her, saying horrible things to her, trying to ruin her marriage and get her fired, working hard to tarnish her reputation. Fortunately, none of that came to fruition, but it was hell for her to live through.

She felt so betrayed. How could her father, whom she had been so close to, attempt to do these things to her? Because that is what sociopaths do. And no matter how much you yearn to have a cozy parent or sibling or friend relationship with them, they are who they are. Ignoring that for the sake of the imagined love and caring one could expect from a healthy person and relationship is emotionally suicidal.

The caller's desire for vengeance was also self-centered: it didn't matter who he'd hurt—until she was the target. This is a kind of selling one's soul for the fantasy of being special.

Sometimes we think we should be special no matter how little we do to earn or deserve it. In fact, our arrogance about believing that and counting on it leads us to push someone into betraying us. I wrote *The Proper Care and Feeding of Husbands* because I saw that the feministas had really poisoned the minds of women against being their husband's girlfriends and lovers, and they needed to be brought back into the reality of how simple it is to have a happy husband and marriage.

Many women discover one day that their husbands have decided they no longer love them and are leaving and/or having an affair. Girlfriends and families close in quickly to reassure these astonished women experiencing the great betrayal of vows. At first, it is usually not handled very well, as the woman becomes an instant emotional wreck—which is understandable.

Then there is usually a lot of crying, yelling, being nasty, threatening (especially about children), and so forth. Just amazingly, temper tantrums rarely make the other person feel warmer toward you.

In *The Proper Care*, I point out that there are several possible scenarios. In one, the spouse is a narcissistic jerk, in which case all bets are off . . . sorry. In another, he is going through some terrible problem and attempting to minimize humiliation and maximize ego by withdrawing and having some hussy adore him. And finally, it might be that the wife has been pushing away a perfectly good man by her lack of care.

So instead of seeking vengeance based on an assumption of betrayal, a wise woman will analyze which of the scenarios best fits her situation. If he is a narcissist, she didn't choose wisely. If he is in emotional trouble, compassion and psychological or medical treatment may be helpful. If he is being pushed away by a lack of a wife's affection, attention, and respect . . . she has all the power to make it better.

One woman in this predicament wrote me that she decided on a form of vengeance: to wake up the very next day and decide to be a better wife. After close to a year of them being horrible to each other, she woke up early one day before her husband and got his stuff ready for work, made him his snack for the day. When he woke up and came into the kitchen, before he could say anything nasty, she asked what kind of drink he wanted with his snack. He was so caught off guard that instead of some unpleasant retort, he hesitatingly said he'd like a Diet Coke. He mumbled a "Thanks," and went through the door stupefied, obviously not sure how to act.

She decided right then and there to make the choice to be happy and kind, and nothing he might say or do would make her be a fishwife anymore.

It is interesting that until that moment, she'd seen herself as helpless in a drowning situation. Now she realized how much power she had over her actions.

The long-term impact was that when she started behaving in a respectful way, so did he. It takes two people to argue, and it's hard for someone to be nasty to you when you are being as sweet as pie. Her marriage was saved by two people who realized taking small angers out on each other (mini-revenges) was not as fulfilling as simply being *nice*.

Ultimately, the point of this chapter has been for you to examine yourself more honestly before you hit the red revenge button. Determine if you really need to accept responsibility for the situation because of your lack of kindness, compassion, understanding, choices, decisions, behaviors, and so forth.

The story that most resonates on that point is one from a young woman who was working at the first job she ever really loved with a nonprofit arts organization. Getting hired by this organization was a bright spot at a very depressing time for her. She was finally in a relationship with someone whom she thought exhibited all that she wanted in a spouse; yet there were signs that the relationship was ending. The complete and total heartache over this consumed her, and she didn't know how to get over it. She admitted to being miserable and miserable to be around. And this all happened within the first three months at her new job.

She eventually pulled it together and pressed on with life, only to be blindsided by an anonymous enemy. Someone had taken information off her journal Web site and forwarded the journal entries to the heads of all the separate entities that made up the large nonprofit. She was suspended without pay while they determined if she had violated any company policies, and subsequently fired. She had just signed a new lease on an apartment and was in the last few months of an advanced education program that had to be finished, but was being denied unemployment due to the reasons for which she had been terminated. Yikes.

While the identity of her attacker is still unknown, she figures it was a prior employee who had been fired herself several months prior to this incident. Of course, my listener wanted revenge—this person had wrecked her life!

"I wanted to hurt her. I wanted to bust the windows in her car, slash her tires, and vandalize her house. I had friends offering to sleep with her boyfriend and wreck her life, but at some point, I had to take some responsibility for my contributions to the situation."

My listener decided that this horrible woman actually did her a favor. In the midst of the attacker's rantings on my listener's Web page, she wrote, "She walks around the office like she's something special. She thinks she's all that but she's nothing but a poor black chick from the projects who hasn't been anywhere and isn't going anywhere."

My listener reflected on that statement—in spite of the incidental point of her never having lived in the projects. She thought back on the days when she first began at her job, and realized how miserable she was about her own personal life. This attacker woman would walk into the office every morning, flitting from office to office with a huge smile, saying, "Good morning," and my listener would respond with barely a grunt. She realizes now that the other woman read her bad attitude as conceit and arrogance. Her attacker felt my listener thought she was better than her, when the truth was that she was just miserable because of her love-life failure.

So instead of invoking her right to some kind of revenge, she decided to let the situation go. A judge thought she had a solid civil case for the harassment, but she didn't want to spend any more time trying to get back at that woman. She consciously *chose* to *learn* from the situation and to think about how she could leave this situation as a better person.

The following are the useful lessons she learned:

Lesson 1: Don't take another person's negative behavior toward you personally. You have no idea what's going on in her world.

Lesson 2: Don't put personal information in a public forum for anyone and everyone to see.

Lesson 3: Don't allow your personal problems to make you into someone that no one wants to be around.

Good lessons to be learned by all.

Chapter Three

Vengeance Is Mine

The vengeance I ask and cry,

By way of exclamation,

On all the whole nation

Of cats wild and tame:

God send them sorrow

and shame!

—John Skelton

I've daydreamed often about how to get back at or hurt my betrayers. Trust me, I've thought of illegal and immoral actions that I hoped would bring great emotional pain and public humiliation to the folks who, for various reasons coming from their own dark recesses or superficial characters, made it a point to betray me. Thinking back as hard as I can, I can't remember a time I ever followed through. Damn.

The "illegal" and "immoral" part always seems to put a sag in my sails. I can only be the kind of person I am, and I am not the kind of person who would do the things I dream about. Damn.

I believe in payback with every fiber of my being, but I can't bring myself to follow through. I am not a goody-two-shoes at all. I just don't want to be the kind of person I would disdain. When I see that the situation they caused backsplashed on them in some deleterious way, I am delighted. But the thing about most "bad" people, betrayers, is that they are like roaches: no matter how much you spray them or try to squash them, they live to scurry another day.

My daydreams of vengeance include such scenarios as:

- They are "outed" as having done the dirty deeds, and everyone scorns and shuns them.

- They come into some terrible trouble (like IRS issues or mold in their home walls), that costs them in time, money, and distress.

- They swallow their own venom and become so consumed with their own meanness that the rest of their lives just collapse.

And my personal favorite:

- Someone betrays them big-time, and they get to suffer the pain and utter helplessness they caused—or continue to cause—me.

Sadly, none of that typically happens. And if my personal favorite happens to them, mean people are able to get almost immediate satisfaction by doing something else devastating, ugly, vulgar, and unbelievably nasty right back—and that makes them feel better.

Therein lies the rub: good people are helpless to some degree in the face of evil and mean because "good" has rules of engagement, while evil and mean are free to do or say whatever they wish without any internal reverberations . . . known as guilt.

True guilt is the awareness that you've breached your own ethical rules of conduct. Guilt is overused by people who feel forced to do something or incur the wrath of another. That is not guilt—it is weakness and fear. Real guilt is a bell going off in your gut that reminds you that you are simply not that kind of person. Only good people feel guilt. Damn.

The betrayals of mine have been mostly public festivals. As I hold a point of view about life and behavior that is considered "conservative," certain portions of our society get a kick out of undermining my ability to communicate that point of view and help people. Because I am successful and visible, some people feel threatened in their positions (even when I have shown absolutely no interest in competing with or replacing them) and attack to maintain their egos. Some people simply want what I have; even though they might admire my hard work, they can't bear that I have or am what they wish.

Some entities just want the profit that comes from being public, embarrassing me without caring one whit whether or not what they're saying is the truth.

I've had television shows bring me on under false pretenses only to try to ambush me for audience excitement and attention—which bring ratings boosts. I mean, the stories go on and on . . . but you get the gist.

I remember one professor I had, a very religious man, who told me early on in my career that his guiding rule was to seem affable to all, but emotionally and socially contain his real world in a small universe around him. Unlike the Mafia model of "keeping your enemies closer than your friends," his advice was to condense your world into a safe, manageable environment. I agree with him.

I have evolved my world into concentric circles where the people I trust completely—who have proven themselves over time, and with whom I have never had one of those moments of doubt—are the closest to me in the center of the circle. Those are the people I can trust, rely on, and count on. These are very few. I have learned to be cautious. And at sixty-three, I no longer have the need to "confide" or "open up" to many as a way of feeling secure in the world.

I have matured over time to understand that everyone has their own story, history, weaknesses, and hidden agendas—whether they even know it or not. I gauge myself carefully in how much of myself I reveal. And frankly, I am emotionally more at peace this way. I have a lot of friends in work and play. These are people I appreciate, enjoy, and admire. We have great times together and good feelings between us. This is possible because I don't burden them—as I was prone to do in my youth—with all my expectations of complete love and loyalty.

As I mentioned in chapter 2, "Betrayal or Not a Betrayal . . . That Is the Question," when your expectations of and for people are out of whack with reality, you yourself create your own sense of hurt and betrayal. Not everyone you know is in the position or of the mindset to be your loyal confidante, who protects your reputation and feelings at all costs to herself. That sort of person is few and far between—and that is as it should be. Scarcity gives certain things their value.

I have suffered publicly and privately because of betrayals of faith, trust, and truth. There have been innumerable occasions when I've wanted to just ditch everything and go hide somewhere. I remember one distinct time after an interview on a national morning television cable show when the well-known cohost

A friend is a person with whom you can be sincere . . . to whom you never need to defend yourself . . . on whom you can depend whether present or absent . . . with whom you never need to pretend . . . to whom you can reveal yourself without fear of betrayal . . . who does not feel she owns you because you are her friend . . . who will not selfishly use you because she has your confidence. I would have such a friend . . . and I would be such a friend. I do have such a friend! = You

—Alfred Montapert

said (and I paraphrase closely), "Aren't you an abusive mother?"

"What?" was my stunned response.

"Aren't you an abusive mother? Isn't it abusive for you to put your son through the humiliation of all the public attacks on you?"

I tell you, if this had not been a remote broadcast, I fear I would have smashed her face silly. That crossed the line. Here she was flaming with innuendos and false accusations and then saying that I was hurting my family by being the brunt of these media shenanigans for ratings and attention.

I took a breath and then said, "My son understands what happens to people who stand up for their principles. He is most proud and supportive of me."

Nonetheless, I felt sick. I certainly don't want to hurt my baby and make life tougher for him. That night I sat down with my son and my husband and told them how badly I felt that my name and character were being dragged through the mud, much of which was splashing onto them. I offered to quit my work, move away, have my son change his name . . . kind of what happens in a witness protection program. My husband just shook his head no. My son stood up, at the grand age of about ten or eleven, put his hands on his hips, and said, "I didn't raise my mother to be a weenie."

As I mentioned, *Saturday Night Live* had "spoofed" me—but by using my son in a most vulgar way. It made me sick inside. *Law & Order* and *The West Wing* had story lines which included a radio talk show host dealing with psychology who had no credentials, in spite of the fact that I am licensed in the state of California as a marriage and family therapist; public record ignored. One of my favorite shows, *Frasier*, did a story line having to do with me and my "crazy mother." This all made me sick inside also.

The motivations for those shows to misrepresent and humiliate me was simply my support of marriage as a special commitment between a man and a woman, and that children are best served by having a mommy and daddy, married and stable. Somehow, those subjects have become controversial, and advocates of such notions are targeted for destruction.

I then sat and read accumulated e-mails from listeners and callers who felt that I had been an important influence, helping them to improve and enjoy their lives. I hung on to the reality that I had a mission, and the test of my character was sticking to that mission in spite of attempts to have me cave, crawl away, or explode into oblivion. It is these folks who should really matter to me. And they do. And that's why I'm still here.

*L*ife shrinks or expands
in proportion to one's courage.

—Anaïs Nin

Hopefully there is something to the cliché that living well is the best revenge. As a matter of fact, direct vengeance is a risky act. Direct revenge feeds people who basically live off the emotional upset of others. I remember one of the original *Star Trek* television series episodes where an unseen force was wreaking havoc with the crew by making them angry. Captain Kirk finally figured out that the evil entity lived off the hateful, negative energy it helped produce. This negative energy was its oxygen and major nutrient. So he had the whole crew constantly laughing. The entity, frustrated and starving, went away. Happy ending.

In real life, though, being happy and living well only sometimes has the desired effect of making betrayers let up; sometimes they become so obsessed with hating and hurting you that it becomes their own reason for living, in spite of the fact that you are clearly emotionally and psychologically removed from it all.

As I did, you have to decide that in spite of outside efforts to the contrary, you can have a good life by your own design and what you choose to focus on. I choose to focus on my opportunities to help others deal with the realities of life and their inner demons.

Don't always count on the people who should step up to protect and support you to do so. But do count on the fact that so-called "good" people have to live with the knowledge that they are weak and will basically stand for nothing. However, after a while they don't even mind that awareness, because their lives are peaceful. This cowardice is a betrayal of values, justice, friendship, and truth.

This seems a good time to look at the difference between justice and revenge. One of the typical arguments about revenge and justice is a misunderstanding of the biblical injunction of "an eye for an eye." That is often incorrectly interpreted as suggesting that if someone takes out your eye, you can turn around and take theirs out. Wrong. It means that there are limits to justice or vengeance. You cannot take out both eyes when only one eye was lost originally. While I'm obviously being too literal in counting eyeballs, the point is that the Bible declares that consequences for a wrong act cannot be greater than the original insult or assault; in fact, they can be much less, especially if there are mitigating circumstances.

This issue of mitigating circumstances often becomes abused with the introduction of bad childhoods, alcoholism, and such, where the assumption is made that your past or your circumstances forced you to

I wanted to change the world.
But I have found that the
only thing one can be sure of
changing is oneself.

—Aldous Huxley

do something you ordinarily wouldn't do. I only re-
serve that argument for a gun to your head—and even
then . . .

There was a fascinating movie about this very prin-
ciple entitled *Nick of Time*. It starred Christopher
Walken (bad guy) and Johnny Depp (good guy). Our
hero is a single dad. His six-year-old daughter is kid-
napped by the bad guys, who threaten to kill his daughter if he doesn't assassinate a senator. This seems simple
enough a predicament for a loving father: kill the senator. But he risks the life of his daughter to sabotage the
assassination plan because one life (his daughter's) is
just as precious as another life (the senator's). He man-
ages to save both his daughter and the senator.

Now, I can see this plot turning out differently with
today's television mentality. Johnny Depp kills the senator, saves his daughter, and his defense attorney gets
him off on some ridiculous plea bargain: "What father
could function otherwise under such pressure?"

Poop. People can do the right thing no matter what
the pressures when they have the courage of their principles. A gun was at Depp's screen daughter's head, and
he still did the right thing. Just fairyland? I hope not.

Justice served righteously can contain revenge, but
revenge is not supposed to be the motivation. Justice is
a social and legal term that has the point of protecting

society and its individuals, as well as controlling relationships between people. If a society has clearly defined expectations of permissible behavior and then stands behind it with courts and sentences, the hope is that fairness between individuals and their protection is assured; consequences are reasonable (criminal court), and attempts will be made to compensate the victim for his hurt (civil court).

Justice is supposed to be formal and devoid of emotion, so it will be respected by all in the community. Passion is at the very core of vengeance.

Passion often leads us to respond out of proportion to the hurt. It can consume us forever, distract us from the beauty and opportunities our lives are still capable of enjoying, and lead to countervengeance—think the Hatfields and the McCoys, or the families of Romeo and Juliet.

One listener wrote that she used the justice system to exact revenge . . . interesting. She sued her ex-husband's new wife for "alienation of affection." It took five years to get the case to court, and a jury had to be selected, but she eventually won her case and was awarded damages. It had taken her almost two years to get divorced, and she suffered lots of humiliation.

She felt that it was all worth it because she let her children know that she was ready to stand up for right and wrong and that vows mean something. The values she had instilled in them were compromised by her husband's (their father's) adultery, and she just would not stand for that betrayal of her children by their dad. The court's decision, while in her favor, was never financially realized because the new wife declared bankruptcy. Nonetheless, her case caused alienation of affection to be placed on the law books in Mississippi, and others have followed suit.

Her ex-husband and his new honey have no money and have been publicly shamed. Justice and vengeance; I like it. But it's not so easy to attain.

Vengeance is justice smothered in passion. It is sometimes an attempt to right a wrong, most times to simply cause as much (or more) hurt as was received. Many people believe that vengeance will bring them peace. I recently had a circumstance that proved that wrong—for me, anyway.

A betrayer got slapped down—not for what she'd done to me for many years straight but for breaking a rule in that venue in which she wove her web of nastiness. I wasn't jubilant—and that surprised me. I realized that whether or not she was in gear in her mean machine, my life was ultimately of my doing, as were my behaviors, my friends, my work, my hobbies, and so forth. Here she was defanged for a while . . . and it really was irrelevant to my life. I figured she'd paint herself a victim in her own mind and in public, and she would live to betray truth and kindness another day. And I said to myself something I've said to many callers, "So what??"

Her getting "slapped" was no vengeance for me and had no meaning to me. My life consists of what I allow into it, physically, spiritually, and emotionally. Her slap-down was very freeing to me. It retaught me a lesson that I've known and taught for half a century but sometimes, in the pure emotion of it all, forget: "The moon is not bothered by the baying of wolves."

So now I look at it this way: my vengeance is that she is consumed with hurting me—and I no longer give her a moment's thought. She is stuck with herself—and I'm no longer stuck with her in any way that counts. Cool.

While I still adore the concept of vengeance—as do just about all of you, or Mafia movies would never be so popular—it is difficult to attain without tarnishing the self. One listener wrote to me that she was talking one day with her best girlfriend, sharing her plan to wreak havoc on someone's life as righteous revenge for that person's betrayal of her, when her girlfriend said, "If you are going to do this, I could no longer be your friend. You are a woman of integrity and self-respect, and as your best friend, I would not allow you to lower yourself to his level."

Ouch on toast!

Listen, bad guys win . . . a lot; fact of life. But ultimately, they *are* bad guys, and you're not. You've got to take solace from that and move on without striking out at everyone and anyone as a kind of faux vengeance. So quit the being paranoid that all people are creeps (they're not), or that if you keep everyone at bay, you won't get hurt (you're hurting yourself). There are better ways of handling issues of vengeance, and I will lead you to that promised land in chapter 4, "Revenge Is Sweet?"

Revenge Is Sweet?

Just my vengeance complete,

The man sprang to his feet,

Stood erect, caught at

God's skirts, and prayed!

So, I was afraid!

—Robert Browning

I love it when I'm ready to write a chapter or section on some subject and I hear, see, read, or experience something that is just right on point. It feels like some mystical support. A few days ago I took a fifteen-minute break before taking on some task or other, and watched the last two segments of a *Law & Order: Criminal Intent* episode that, as it surprisingly turned out, was decidedly about revenge.

Here's the plot, as I guessed: high-profile, extremely wealthy man and woman, married, have split up due to his affairs. Additionally, when he dumped her rudely and without financial resources, he also stole millions that were in a bank account; the number of that account was written in a "cheat book" that his musician friend carried with him everywhere.

The husband was in jail, charged with the murder of said musician; however, the wife refused to testify, and therefore there would not be enough evidence to convict . . . so he is set free. She has invited her ex to her meager apartment to "bring their marriage back," and has some fabulous wine and two glasses ready for their toast to each other.

The two detectives knock on the door and enter the room. One of the detectives is absolutely certain the man did not kill his friend . . . and the monologue as he closes in on the truth is tremendously intriguing.

The detective starts painting a picture of a wronged and abandoned woman who had no intention of really getting back *with* her ex, but did intend to get back *at* him. He said she killed the musician friend to get the book with the ID number for the bank account with the stolen or hidden millions. The detective continued by suggesting that she set the ex-husband up to come to her by telling him that he needed her now that she had the ID number.

Then the detective picked up the bottle of wine and poured the contents into one glass. The vintage was strange; ash and the metal spiral of a burned notebook.

Still, the woman won't admit to anything, repeating time and time again that she is not the kind of person who could kill anybody (evidently there were other murders in her plot of revenge). The detective keeps holding up in front of her eyes a photo of what she looked like before the divorce: lovely, happy, cheerful, and decent. He keeps pushing her to get back into that place . . . and eventually she breaks and starts screaming at her ex-husband, ending up with the proclamation, "Look what you've done to me. Look what you've turned me into."

The detectives handcuff her and lead her out of the apartment. The ex-husband hangs his head in his hands until he is cuffed and also led out for admitting to the theft.

The millions of dollars will stay somewhere in financial oblivion. Both the exes will spend the rest of their lives in jail.

But the part I want to discuss was the harping of the detective on what kind of person she was now and how she needed to take responsibility for her actions, because the old her would want her to do that. She started to decompensate: sobbing and hand-wringing and almost an outside-of-herself transformation as she moved away from her justifiable anger at her ex and got in touch with what she had given up in her soul and life by getting her revenge. She was right . . . he was devastated to lose the money. She was wrong . . . she gave up her soul and the lives of other people to get that moment of taking from him what he wanted the most: money.

And . . . it wasn't worth it in the end.

But what if she had never killed anybody? That plot line stacked the deck against the concept of the potential value of revenge by taking it to the extreme. Multiple homicides of innocent people aimed at taking away somebody's money to hurt their feelings certainly can never be justified.

What if she had simply stolen the spiral notebook with the bank ID number in it, burned it, and used the ashes to toast her husband and his dreams of living the rest of his life in luxury on some deserted island? I would have whooped with delight and thrown her a party.

That would have been worth it in the end. Why? It would have been worth it because it did not require her to sell her soul or bring misery to innocent people and their families. The end result was that his worship of money and bimbos would have backfired on him. Works for me!

Electricity is neither bad nor good—it just is. It can light up a city, bring warmth to a home, and allow for cooking dinner. Or you could stick your finger in a socket and get electrocuted. If you were so foolish or careless as to misuse electricity, it certainly would not be the electricity's fault, would it?

Well, look at revenge in the same way. Someone can break moral and civil rules and laws to get back at somebody who betrayed her. Or, she could not break moral and civil rules, and still give a betrayer some appropriate F. And, risking your disapproval, dear reader, I'm all for that.

Let's go back to *Law & Order*'s final comment from the ex-wife. She yelled ferociously at her ex-husband; she said that he'd made her into what she became: a cold-blooded murderer who had sacrificed her soul and her life to hurt a man who betrayed her financially and through infidelity.

He did not make her do any of that. He hurt her, betrayed her, screwed her over financially, and left her destitute, and was quite cavalier about it—that is all true. This did not dictate her response. His horrendous behaviors were not the architect of her atrocious reactions. While we can't control the world, we do have control over our actions and decisions. We choose our path; we choose our responses; we choose to stay in the character we would most respect.

All those true stories of women being wronged and dumped, coming back to murder and create mayhem, do not make me feel any sympathy for the woman at all!

The type of vengeance we choose to administer is a window into our character and a building block for our souls.

The odd thing about revenge is how it doesn't always produce the hoped-for emotion. Early in my radio career, for one great big fat example from my own life, someone selfishly took something from me, something dear, and then destroyed it by virtue of their hubris.

A colleague at my radio station was jealous of my rising career and got me fired by threatening to leave during her contract negotiations. As she was well established in her time slot at that point, management finally acquiesced to her demand. The head of the sales department came to tell me the truth with great sadness, as I was well liked personally and appreciated for my work.

It took me years to get back to a major station. During this time her star continued to fade. When I finally got the opportunity to have a national show, she decided to compete with me with her own show, and she failed, after being quite public about her superiority to me.

To my own surprise, I didn't feel the elation one would imagine or that I had anticipated, as I knew this person would fail. In fact, I felt kind of let down. I've been cogitating over this, trying to figure out why I wasn't going in circles with high-fives, and in fact felt sad instead.

I am a big believer in revenge, as I've already mentioned several times. I love movies where there is serious payback: "Hooray, one for the good guys!" I cheer inside and out loud when somebody who hurt another "gets theirs" in a big way. It makes the world seem right somehow. When we're little, to manipulate us into being good kids, parents tell us all sorts of clichés about how bad doesn't pay and good always has the big payoff. As we get older, we see that whistleblowers get fired and do-gooders get exploited, and our sense of reality gets turned upside down and inside out. So, to have renditions that match our childlike fantasies of what is "right is right" is a great relief and uplift.

But I didn't feel either when this person had to munch on crow. And I kept wondering, Why? All I can come up with is that in the final analysis it just didn't matter. I had to get on with my life, and did so with the help and love of a number of friends and colleagues. And get on I did; with new challenges and experiences that, frankly, weren't there when I had what was taken. Oddly, a number of aspects of my life improved dramatically; fundamental was that I was being treated with more respect and given more support. My "emotional" situation had improved significantly. So, in many ways, when the dirty deed was done to me, another door opened that was more personally pleasant.

As time passed, my anger and hurt subsided as I became more invested in the changed elements of my life and expanded my activities. I filled the time with things other than thoughts of payback, things other than hopes of karma, things other than hopes of great comeuppance.

As I write, I always come to understand myself better. I still love revenge, but it isn't always necessary for any of us to have a good life. When betrayed, I am at first furious beyond measure, wishing for a gladiator to rise up and wipe that person's smirk off the face of the earth. And then . . . I just don't care. I have too much good in my life to care.

Mourning is the process by which we let go. I realized I could and would simply let go of any remnants of rage, pain, delightful wishes of great pain, and any other attachment—all of which are obviously negative. That "letting go" is an odd "letdown." It is over. It is finished. That book is closed, and I have the rest of my life to enjoy and prosper. Call that forgiveness, if you will. . . . I just call it letting go of one end of the cesspool to swim over to the other side and get into a wonderful swimming pool.

Unfortunately, some people get stuck in not wanting to let go of the dream of devastating their betrayer. It

You don't want to dwell on your enemies, you know. I basically feel so superior to my critics for the simple reason that they haven't done what I do.

—John Irving

becomes an obsession. Why? Because it is easier to hate than move on—simple as that. Hate requires nothing but rehashing the story and stoking the fire to keep the flame of rage alive. It is hating instead of living.

From my point of view, that is tantamount to becoming your own betrayer.

Revenge is supposed to be an endpoint, not a change of address to purgatory. One female listener wrote to me of her understandable hurt and shame that her husband had cheated on her after thirty years of marriage. She only found out about this because he ended up giving her a sexually transmitted disease.

She forgave him, not wanting to lose her marriage at this point in her life. Well, she appeared to forgive him. In truth, she wrought vengeance each and every day by withholding sex, warmth, conversation, and any semblance of marital harmony, as she slept in a separate bedroom. This went on for three months, until she ended up at a doctor's office, diagnosed with mild depression.

This led her to actually talk with her husband . . . in depth. She realized that she said she had forgiven him, but she really hadn't. She was doing everything in her power to punish him and ended up feeling worse. So she told him this would stop. She understood that she had to really, really forgive him and move on—or end up on some happy pills. She chose to move on, and now they are getting along wonderfully.

Sometimes people stick with surreptitious forms of revenge because they haven't developed their inner core strength to confront people and situations directly. One listener wrote that in junior high school she was very shy and was bullied by a number of girls who would pull down her skirts/shorts, make fun of her, tease her, keep her from sitting with them at lunch, and so forth.

The teachers trusted her, and she was given responsibilities such as access to locker combinations, which the office aide had to help students who had forgotten their combinations. Her style of revenge was to get the combinations for the girls who picked on her, open their lockers, and tear up their prized pictures of their boyfriends or mess up something that was meaningful to them.

In her pained adolescent mind, she'd found great satisfaction in the "harmless" punishment. Looking back, some twenty years later, she still has pleasure at the memories. She reflected on being too shy to ever voice her pain and still considers the destruction of these girls' property to be a harmless outlet for her anguish. She'd never gotten the respect and acceptance she so desperately wanted, and this was her way to feel some power.

From the viewpoint of an adolescent, this is understandable. From the viewpoint of an adult, this so-called harmless outlet for anguish is a trap. Not being able to speak up for oneself and learn to connect in a healthy way to others, and instead to needle them with mysterious annoyances, does not in any way aid in well-being in any meaningful way. One's life becomes focused on pursuing these minuscule moments of grandeur—none of which change anything in the world or in your life. Each time you sneak to prick somebody else's life, you fixate yourself in that mode of mouse.

Either stand up for yourself—or move on. Those are the only two means of growth.

A man wrote to me about the small landscaping business in New Jersey he had as a twenty-four-year-old. It seems that a customer cheated him out of over a thousand dollars in payment for yard work. At first he used the check-in-the-mail lie. Then he moved over to, "I don't have the money." After this young man suggested a payment schedule, it was, "Hey, it is a part of business to sometimes not get paid. Chalk it up as a loss. When you grow up, you'll get it."

Well, grow up he did. And five years later he passed a huge sign with the names of some people running for town council. Yup, among the names was that of the deadbeat. He was furious that a guy who couldn't or wouldn't handle his own finances would dare to imagine he could run a town's finances.

When he got off from work that day, he drove around town defacing each and every poster with the words *deadbeat, cheapskate,* and *crook* under this guy's photo. Somebody must have seen him, because the police called him in. He owned up to doing it, much to the police officer's surprise, and then told him why. He also got a call from the local newspaper, who'd interviewed that "deadbeat"—who was making a living as a financial adviser—and wanted his story. There were a lot of follow-up editorials in the paper slamming his former client, and he ended up dropping out of the race and left town altogether within the year.

Our "perp" got a $200 fine in front of a courtroom full of people who gave him applause after he told his story to the judge.

I think this was more than appropriate, as that man was obviously not of the character to serve the public. This revenge served the public good.

Revenge that directly helps others is benevolent! One recent listener wrote about her love affair of one year—which she kept going in her mind for another nineteen years, imagining she still loved him. Well, a year into this relationship he broke up with her, giving her no reason. He soon started dating another woman (oops, the reason!). However, he would continually call and leave messages on her voice mail—messages she saved for almost a year.

One night she came up with the idea to forward all these messages to the girlfriend. The messages included saying he loved and missed her, wished they would work things out, hoped she didn't hate him, and so forth. He even called her on Christmas morning, leaving a message while on his way to his girlfriend's mother's house for dinner.

My listener and the girlfriend met for coffee. They went together to confront him, and he denied it all . . . until, of course, she played the tapes.

That saved the girlfriend from a stupid decision to date this guy. However, my listener admitted that she wished she had not spent so much time and energy over the years on him.

Another woman wrote me about her accounting education at a midwestern university. The head of the accounting department also happened to be her professor for an entry-level accounting course. To make a long story short, he gave her the option of failing the class or meeting him at his home for the weekend.

She failed the course and had to spend two years working around this failure before she could finally get back on track. She'd never told anyone—just worked the channels to attain her goal. On that last registration day, lo and behold, who is sitting at the desk? The professor! She walked up to him, and he greeted her in a congenial manner. When he asked her, "How are you doing?" she responded with, "Well, I'm seven credits short in accounting, but I would be willing to fail seven thousand times before doing what you insisted in order for me to pass your class."

"A pin could have dropped," she wrote. "There was nobody in that lineup of students nor in the entire staff who did not clearly understand my meaning. It was much better than any juristic court action could have rewarded me. By the way, I teach banking and finance now at a European university. I include special insights in my lessons, promoting students to stand up for what is 'right' not only in student experience, but in the work world."

I have often told people to do just what she did: in public make a statement that is short, sweet, and to the point in its revelation of exploitation, threats, bullying, or harassment. The truth is out in a clean manner—not immoral, illegal, or fattening. Just what I prescribe.

However, there are those who choose to have revenge in a more ferocious manner. One woman, married to a soldier and stationed in Okinawa, decided to get back at her abusive husband by being—abusive.

She bought a huge jar of hot peppers, drained the juice, soaked all his underwear in it, and dried them. Okinawa has extremely hot weather, and wearing military fatigues makes it even hotter. He wore these shorts for four days and ended up in sick bay, looking like he'd been scalded. They gave him some medication, and it healed. After two weeks she did it again.

"As you can see," she wrote, "I can and will get even. I divorced about a year later, and I have been married to a wonderful man for thirty-five years now."

I was actually shocked by this, as she caused physical harm to her husband instead of (a) reporting his abuse to his superiors and (b) seeking refuge and leaving.

This to me is not self-defense—which would be to physically defend herself, call the military police, or go home to mother. Staying there to stick it to him is a provocative and dangerous ploy with an already violent man.

To this day she is pleased with her actions. I believe they were dangerous and juvenile . . . but make a funny story three decades later.

Of course, many stories are amusing in retrospect. One woman's ex-husband cheated on her with a mutual friend after years of being critical, controlling, and philandering. He'd asked her if they could separate so he could decide if he wanted this latest "honey" or her. She said she'd had enough. He moved out of the house and left his large dog, most possessions, and all the other responsibilities of the home behind, to be cared for by her and picked up when he decided that he wanted them back.

One day, while she was looking out at the backyard, realizing that she needed to clean it up due to the mounting doo-doo, she went to his motorcycle helmet and found his very expensive leather riding gloves. She carefully put them on and proceeded to pick up the dog poop in the backyard. When she had finished, she took the gloves off and put them back in his helmet.

She figured, if he was going to act like a sh*t head, then he might as well really be one.

I am ashamed to tell you I loved this story. LOL.

Another woman wrote that she filed for divorce because her then husband was so emotionally destructive that she was getting migraines. Thinking that he would get back at her for the embarrassment of her dumping him, he decided that he would not move out of the house while he was dating new girls. His plan was to upset her and have her give up assets to get him out. He wouldn't provide finances for the home of four children. Obviously, a scum of a guy.

Our heroine figured out a cute way to get him out of the home. While he was in Las Vegas for a week with some honey, she decided all reasoning with him was futile. When her husband arrived "home," he was met by four thrilled children holding a cuddly kitten they had all just adopted at the local ASPCA. Oh-oh. He was allergic, highly allergic, to cat fur.

She wrote, "Sometimes—although counterproductive—revenge can sometimes help. I truly believe that this was one of the few times in my life that it actually did. He moved out the very next week. Our family is happily divorced from the turmoil that was."

She is obviously happy about getting back control over her own life. I don't consider the kitten an act of revenge; I consider the kitten *checkmate*.

I just love examples of stupid revenge. One woman had dated a young man for three months when out of the blue he told her he had a girlfriend who was going to be visiting him from out of state for two weeks, and he didn't want the other girlfriend to know about her. As this woman was not exactly mean-spirited, she thought of a humorous plot of revenge.

The night the out-of-town girlfriend arrived, this woman and her friend decorated his car as "Just Married," complete with a bag of rice poured all over the interior, baby booties hanging on the rearview mirror, miniature marshmallows all over the windows except for a heart for the driver to peer through, washable poster paint with hearts, streamers from the antenna, cans dragging behind. Evidently, by morning the marshmallows had puffed up, and it took eleven car washes to clean his car.

"That Sunday," she wrote, "he and his girlfriend were congratulated over the pulpit at church. They received three wedding gifts, which he had to return. He got the clear message that I wasn't going to play his game with a little humor mixed in."

Frankly, I like this "revenge" too.

And then there is the case of the woman scorned who filled out every insert card in every magazine she could find with the name of the "other woman," and put a check mark by "bill me later." She did this for a solid year.

"Was it juvenile?" she wrote. "Yes. Did it make me feel better? You bet!"

Frankly, I like this revenge too.

Okay, silliness aside, these few "pranks" are light revenge; they don't really damage anybody, just cause enough annoyance to give the doer a little surge of power and glee.

However, that is not typically what revenge looks like, and throwing water always gets the thrower wet. When one husband cheated on his wife, she got revenge by sleeping with his best friend.

"Wasn't worth the trouble. The guy was bad in bed, and sleeping with him didn't make me feel any better about my husband. Just reinforced that men are pigs."

Reading this made me so sad. She hurt herself. She colluded with her betrayer to make herself feel less. That breaks my main rule about revenge: Don't let it cast a shadow on your soul and very being.

In conclusion, this brief comment from a listener of my radio program: "My dad is the type of person who thrives on revenge. He actually feels good about it. Once I had a bad relationship with a boyfriend and exacted minor revenge on him when splitting up. At first, while doing it, I felt good. But immediately afterward I didn't feel good with myself. That was an important lesson for myself: how revenge will never satisfy me."

To quote Dick Armey, "You can not get ahead while you are getting even." So, while I still adore the concept of revenge, I'd rather have a nice day.

Chapter Five

A Philosophical Approach to Revenge

The problem is not that there are problems. The problem is expecting otherwise and thinking that having problems is a problem.

—Theodore Rubin

Yesterday was an incredibly beautiful day. It was the first day of the three-day President's Day weekend. I got up early and had a wonderful breakfast. After that I came down to my office and finished the chapter before this one, "Revenge Is Sweet?" I then showered and put on all my Harley gear and, waiting for my husband to get ready (who says women are slower at that?), I finished up weaving a scarf for our Mother's Day on-line (www.drlaura.com) sale to raise funds for the Wounded Warriors Foundation.

We got on our bikes and rode in a cool breeze and under a clear, sunny sky. Stopping off at a lovely little village right on the ocean, we ate lunch at a fabulous restaurant where I splurged my week's fat allowance on the best onion rings this side of the moon. We then walked through the small local shops, I bought a bunch of great hand-dyed yarn, and we rode back home.

As I was about to mount my Harley, I thought for a moment about how delightful the day had been. And it occurred to me that I was unbelievably happy and content with my life . . . in spite of those who've spited me. That moment was transcendent. I was glad at that moment to be me and not them—the wind wasn't blowing past their helmets as they cruised the road. I love my life, and I've worked hard to make it what it is. And—I could have a day like today no matter what garbage has been thrown at me or what rug has been pulled out from under me.

That is a philosophical approach to revenge. It is only because I realize this and am living it that I feel qualified to write this book for you. Additionally, I have spent thirty-three-odd years (some of them were odd!) on the radio talking to people whose lives have been derailed for protracted amounts of time, less by the betrayer than by their own lack of a philosophical approach in dealing with the slings and arrows that definitely get aimed at every living person.

Some people won't rest without having "taken out" the bad guys. A father of one of my listeners (six-time Purple Heart winner and war hero) told her that for the first time in her life he was disappointed with her. He was ashamed that she allowed evil to win. "You never let the bad guy win," he said.

Instead of taking on the bully—the manager of a famous presidential library, no less—she'd decided to quit her job. Well, it became a toss-up as to which hurt her more: the bullying from the manager or the biting criticism from her father. There's no happy ending to this brief story . . . sorry.

Sometimes it is just all bad, and you don't have much power to flip things in your favor. That's exactly why you have to figure out a way to put it all away, or life progressing toward luxurious moments of delirious happiness will never happen.

Miraculously, on rare occasions, the betrayer bad guy/gal will flip 180 degrees! It is rare . . . but when the evildoer ultimately gets out that microscope and finds his or her conscience, things can turn to the incredible.

One ex-military listener had just that experience. The chief engineer in her unit was brutal to her. She was counting the days until this chief would have a transfer—but that was five more months of torture! One night she and the chief stood four hours of watch after having done a full day's work. The chief over-heard her talking to her parents, giving them direc-tions for the delivery of her expressed breast milk. The parents were at her home for four days to celebrate her birthday and see the grandkids.

The chief told her to go home. After that night, everything seemed to change. Some time later they met up by accident at a bus stop in France (the ship had just started a two-month NATO exercise). Believe it or not, the chief apologized and explained that she had hated her at first sight and wanted to punish her. It turns out that the chief was a lesbian and envied her for her husband, her children, and her Naval Academy education.

Imagine that: an apology with complete clarification and a quite intimate admission of inner turmoil. Not only that, but this chief went on to recommend her for important promotions. Now this is not a typical story. For this kind of happy ending you need a basically decent person whose conscience ultimately does not allow them their evil deeds. Even when the evildoer is "basically decent," defensiveness, saving face, and ego usually diminish any urge to make things right.

Right before he died, the former mentor I mentioned who'd used the nude photos of me to attempt a rekindling of his celebrity (and punish me for mine) told a third party that he wished he hadn't done to me what he did. Of course, he didn't make the admission public, as he had made the betrayal, because his ego just wouldn't allow it. When I heard about his admission, I thought,

"Good—he feels bad . . . and feeling that you are bad hurts." I was happy that he found some part of his soul, and, frankly, happy that he hurt over something that he had done several years prior. He deserved to hurt. That it came from within himself was a surprise to me. All I'd done to retaliate was to survive him.

While my listener got philosophical in her letter to me about never letting herself fall victim to self-pity, and never doing anything she would be ashamed of, " . . . and it paid off," she is absolutely wrong. The turnabout of her chief was not the payoff for her standing strong. Her chief was ashamed inside herself and had the character to remedy her actions, in spite of her powerful jealousies and inner turmoil. My listener could have kept the sweetest demeanor ever, and that wouldn't have changed the heart of the chief . . . that had to come from within herself.

Don't count on sweet and hardworking to manipulate such miracles into being. You don't do sweet and hardworking to change the hearts of the grinches. You do sweet and hardworking to salvage your own life and inner being.

In fact, neither sweet and hardworking nor tearing yourself up inside typically will have any real impact on the perpetrator of the dastardly deeds. The prolonged desire for revenge and justice will just make you crazy inside. You might philosophically lean on the hope, which often comes true, that the universe has a way of equalizing all things. Bad things do not just happen to good people—bad things happen to all people.

So if you wait long enough, your nemesis's turn will come. As one listener put it, "Sooner or later, the inevitable will happen. Your nemesis will be forced to pay in some way. Perhaps their house will burn down, or they will break a leg, their dog will die, or their car will get stolen. Your nemesis will be forced to pay in the currency of grief, pain, fear, sorrow, anger, anxiety, and inconvenience."

While it is "not nice" to wish such tragedies upon anybody, and there is no correlation between their betrayal and such horrid events, be aware that it is not a cosmic payback. It is just their roll of the dice into snake eyes. If you are the sort of person who gloats on the misfortune of others . . . you've lost something inside yourself.

When one woman discovered that her friend was a sociopath, she went on the warpath. She took the betrayer to court and won a judgment—which became useless when the woman filed bankruptcy.

While she benefited immensely by learning a lot about legal work (she filed all her writs herself), she realized that the consequence to her in the mountains of her time and the negative impact the experience had on her emotions wasn't worth the effort. "I believe that vengeance is not usually very helpful, as the stress and sad emotions usually do more self-harm than good under usual circumstances. I was financially and emotionally harmed by taking all of the court action, which lasted far longer than I anticipated. It is so difficult to understand and grasp what some people are capable of doing."

To digress a moment, that last statement is the biggest problem we all have with our betrayers in a nutshell: "what some people are capable of doing." I have been amazed both on the air and in my own life discovering the lengths people will go to simply to hurt somebody for whatever disturbed notions. It is perplexing how some people can freely and comfortably try to destroy others for their own physical or psychological gain. Whether or not we understand it, it still is a force to contend with; a force that, by virtue of evil having little constraint and no rules of engagement, can easily sweep good aside like a tsunami.

A listener wrote of her understanding of her sister's motivations in co-opting the "rehabilitation" of her mentally ill, out-of-control teenage daughter: was it in order—sibling-rivalry style—to prove she was the better mother? No. My listener finally figured out

In order to have an enemy, one must be somebody. One must be a force before he can be resisted by another force.

—Anne Sophie Swetchine

that her sister identified with the potentially homicidal daughter because she had been just like the daughter when she was a teen. Her sister was the one who had climbed out the window and done all the violent and sexual things her daughter was performing. "I realize that if she admits my daughter needed help, it would be like admitting she needed help."

That final awareness hits truth in the center. Understanding of the motivation, however, provides little power and less satisfaction. However, it may be useful if you feel like a strip of flypaper, blaming yourself for the fly droppings in your life. It usually isn't about "getting you" for some deserved punishment; it is usually about getting you for someone else's own disturbed and distorted perceptions and needs.

The knee-jerk feeling of retaliation is an exciting one; it energizes and whips up the adrenaline. The desire to hurt is great. You may fantasize about the betrayer driving along a highway followed by "a half-blind drunken illegal alien on meth driving a jet fuel tanker with bad brakes. I guess that cancels my bid for sainthood," as a listener mused.

While fantasies like that one are a sick kind of "hoot," there are better ways of dealing with the hurt and rage of betrayal. I am going to outline for you some of the better perspectives to take and techniques to follow.

I remember a time, when my career first started, when a radio executive was "unkind behind my back." I believe he was quite irritated that I did not play the "kiss up to sponsor" game so prevalent at that time. Instead of confrontation or all-out war, I simply went to his office, closed the door, and said, calmly and sweetly—showing profound concern for *his* well-being—"Some of the folks you think are trustworthy with your confidences, well, aren't trustworthy. They are reporting to those you talk about the content of your comments. I just wanted you to know you should be more careful whom you trust." And with a sweeter smile, I quietly and softly left his office. I almost fell over with laughter when I got back to my office.

Here he'd been surreptitiously snotty, and now he felt naked. And to any fly on the wall, I was simply being kind. Now that *is* a hoot. It left me giggly with no bad, vengeful, hurt, furious, or ferocious feelings. I felt on top of the world because I had rocked his with apparent kindness. Great moment in history.

There are many times that you and I have lost our cool and gone berserk over things. But what always works out the best is to remain calm and, as one listener wrote, "be vague with my complaints, because I find if you leave out details they can't engage you in a back-and-forth defensive tit for tat . . . plus they already know what they did, and I don't need to tell them." She reminisced about the days when she was eight years old, and a friend turned on her in order to join the popular group.

"When I told my gal-pal I was no longer interested in hanging out, of course she asked why. I told her very calmly and rationally that there were indicators that she was not really being a very good friend to me and that I knew she knew what I meant. If not, maybe she could think of some things she did that were not so nice to me and then realize that somebody ratted her out. The girl was speechless."

My listener then sent her friend whatever belongings had been at her house and just "ate" the $50 worth of her own CDs and clothes at the brat's house. "That fifty dollars was well spent in my mind because I was unleashed from a person doing harm to me."

I was so impressed, reading her e-mail, to realize that at the tender age of eight she had learned such an important concept as disengagement after defanging with such finesse.

One male listener confided about being betrayed by his now ex-wife, who tried to turn their child and all their friends and relatives against him as a smokescreen that barely hid the multiple affairs she'd been having with coworkers. Instead of blowing a gasket or getting outta Dodge, he put on a smiley face. His revenge was to be the kind of man and father that his ex would regret not having and that his daughter would adore. "When I come home, my daughter comes running, yelling, 'Daddy, my daddy!' as loudly as she can. My ex-wife still holds that anger of her own mistakes and is living with shack-up number three since the divorce. My daughter knows the chaos in her mother's shack-up world and spends no less than five to six days a week with me."

By the way, his wife snarls at him constantly that she is sick of seeing him always be the "hero" and "good guy." That is a definite "duh" moment. And every time she says it, it is vindication for daddy.

Daddy transferred his rage at his ex-wife into love for his daughter and has sacrificed any personal/sexual life to focus on her needs and security. Sublimation of ugly feelings into benevolent action is like using poop for fertilizer instead of an assault.

Speaking of imagery, one listener had an amusing way of handling a cruel, bullying boss who was clearly out to get her. Weekly, this boss would call her in for meetings and berate her for imagined transgressions. She delighted in making her squirm and cry. When she asked the boss for specifics (being a type A personality and wanting to be a good girl), the boss would be vague and say, "Well, I just feel . . . that you have a

negative attitude, not as dedicated as you could be . . ."
Nebulous stuff geared to upset.

For a year my listener complained to her friends
and relatives—until they got sick and tired of hearing
it—and was upset all the time. Finally, after listening
to much of my on-air commentary about feelings not
being facts, and how we are not powerful enough to
change someone else's irrational feelings, nor can we
reach into their heads with a psychic screwdriver and
tighten up whatever is loose . . . she had a revelation!
She realized that she was partly responsible for the
boss's power to reach into her head and upset her.

What came from this is hilarious and healthy: "I decided to face those meetings agreeably, with a smile,
knowing that her judgments were 100% wrong. I
stopped letting her into my psyche. In fact, I kept a hilarious mental image in mind: as she talked, I literally
pictured her rolling my severed head back and forth
across the desk blotter, from one hand to the other and
back again. She was 'playing with my head'!"

Residual anger and annoyance don't go away quite
that easily, but if you, as this listener did, train yourself
to *disconnect* emotionally, you can go on with your job,
as reliably as always, with an improved attitude. The
moral to that story is that *nobody can get your goat if
you don't have one.*

You don't *have* to let people into your head; and you don't have to respect their perceptions more than you do your own.

So instead of whining to people, lean on the good ones in your life, because their love, affection, and respect will reassure you. Take from them the goodness you need to reinforce yourself so that you can get back into whatever scene you've probably withdrawn from, be it church, a club, a committee, a family gathering, and so forth.

When people are out to get you, they delight in knowing they forced you into a corner or totally out the door. That's the worst thing for you to let them see, especially when they are but one rotten element in an otherwise okay situation. So, even before you feel strong enough to do so, spiff up, shoulders back, put a smile on your face, and start attending events you've been avoiding out of hurt or misplaced embarrassment with your head held high and your light turned on maximum. This will jump-start your growth in self-confidence, and your increased strength will help you take on all kinds of new experiences because you'll learn to trust your own ability to survive.

As one listener put it, "I guess my revenge was to be beautiful inside and out and let them eat their hearts out that they can't touch me!"

*M*an needs difficulties;
they are necessary for health.

—Carl Jung

Now that is an impressive victory, and it is all *inner* victory—instead of one contrived out of wreaking vengeance directly.

It is your *inner* world that is of greatest significance. What you do with the pain you've been caused is the qualifying event for the Olympic trial of your life. "Even if the cards are massively stacked against you, every minute of depression equals sixty seconds of inaction. I'm not out of the woods yet, but I will be," wrote a male listener. And he is right on. It is natural to spend some time in shock. After all, the reaction to a trauma, physical or emotional, is immediate shock, disbelief, and a horrid awareness of what you just lost. That's normal and natural. I've often said that I permit myself the few days of whining, self-pity, and being pathetic that it takes to get to the next phase—which is an action plan.

Action plans are best made after the philosophical statement is made in your own head. An example of such is a closing line in the movie *Ever After*, when Danielle (Drew Barrymore) tells her stepmother, "After today, I will forget you and never think of you again; but you, I am quite sure, will think of me every day for the rest of your life." "Cinderella" then goes on to live a happy, healthy, and prosperous life with the man of her dreams.

The point is that people who set out to do you evil are generally obsessed and will, even if they can't cause any more damage, think about you forever because you are the "fish that got away." You have to disconnect and come up with an action plan to continue your life in forward gear.

You might jump to new adventures! I am almost glad for betrayals because the upshot is that I have been stirred from a certain amount of habit into finally making sure there is going to be nothing on my Bucket List (from the movie of the same name: two terminally ill men make and fulfill a list of things to do before they "kick the bucket"). I am revving up for my first ocean race, have taken up weaving with a passion, have begun to practice wire-wrapping jewelry making, and look forward to whatever other things I'm going to do.

That is the blessing of some powder-keg explosions—cleaning up their debris often reveals new objects for valuing.

One computer technician got royally screwed over by a competitive coworker and ended up without a job. Here she was at fifty-five years of age with no pension, no 401(k), and only a few thousand in the bank. She has taken on grunt jobs to pay for her first love, which she'd left in a box on top of her life's shelf: art. "It's my love of doing the art that drives me to work hard at my 'day' jobs. I have what I want as far as pursuing my dream—yet financially I have lost so much. It is my vocation as an artist that prevents me from feeling like a complete failure. At the artboard there is just simply me . . . working hard with no excuses."

Sometimes the betrayal in friendship or at work is a kind of cosmic nudge for you to finally pursue what you've put aside. Listen to that voice. Start having the adventures and challenges that can and should no longer wait or just be pipe dreams. Start taking those things off your Bucket List.

Sometimes getting revenge keeps you from moving forward because you lose something or someone precious. One woman, happily married sixteen years with three kids, remembers when she first started dating her husband almost two decades ago. It seems he had just broken up with his girlfriend when they met. After dating about four months, she found out that he'd been communicating with and seeing the old girlfriend on and off behind her back. One night he just broke down and told her. He expressed great remorse and told her that he'd been ambivalent about going back with her— but that he finally had made the decision that the old girlfriend should definitely be an ex-girlfriend.

She broke up with him for a week and then got back together, but that indiscretion of his took a major toll on her and her trust of him. She was devastated by the betrayal and carried around a tremendous amount of hurt and anger for a long, long time. Many times over the years she felt like she wanted to get back at him, to show him how terrible he had made her feel. "But the adult side of me knew I really couldn't go through with that, didn't want to go through with that, and that I couldn't live carrying around the guilt of knowing I did that to him. I never acted on those emotions, and I'm so glad I didn't. He's a great man who made a mistake that he owned up to."

If she had called my show, I would have reminded her that (a) he owned up to his behavior, (b) he'd been confused, (c) he was truly remorseful, and (d) he picked her! I clarify to people in such situations that there is a difference between an "event" and a "pattern." In an event, for which the person is truly sorry, there is room for forgiveness and even a continuation of intimacies. Where there is a pattern, the other person is simply dangerous and destructive, and apologies are manipulations to keep you around to hurt some more.

Revenge in a situation of an "event" would have lost her the prize of a wonderful marriage and family.

Sometimes you just have to sit it out and see if the betrayal really takes on traction. One team coach had to kick off a kid who was very disrespectful, foul-mouthed, and showing up high to practice. His mother, a teacher at the same school, sent around a multipage letter to everyone, full of lies about the coach. What a humiliation! What a threat!

While it might have been justified, instant retaliation would not have given the coach the time to assess the damage. Sometimes you need to stand up—other times, put yourself on the bench and cool down.

That same kid showed up drunk at school a few days later and was suspended.

The coach's reputation was so good to start out with that this attack was swept aside as a hand might shoo a fly.

"My reputation seemed to speak for itself, and this ordeal was soon forgotten by all involved. At the time, I had imagined people would be whispering about it for years to come!"

So, when hit . . . wait. Sometimes that provides the justice.

Direct revenge can cause you to become what you'd least like. One woman wrote of her husband's affair. She was devastated, feeling betrayed, wronged, and unworthy of love. She had her own affair because she felt righteous and entitled to punish him for destroying their love and marriage, and her self-esteem, faith, innocence, and life. "My affair was not worth it, and given another chance, I would never do it again. My affair went against my values and morals, and this event forever changed me as a person. Though I stopped the affair on my own after three months, I learned that I was no better than my husband, that I too, was capable of being dishonest. Revenge served no purpose and just caused additional grief and chaos. Revenge prolonged the healing."

Taking direct revenge most often will leave you feeling like you've betrayed yourself.

A more philosophical approach is definitely the way to go. One woman wrote me of an *Animal Cops* television broadcast that depicted a little dog in horrible condition, being rescued from the most awful abuse imaginable; trembling, terrified, and never having experienced a moment of kindness in her life.

"Six months later, cleaned up and settled in a loving new home, this dog was the picture of happiness. She didn't carry her past—or any sadness about it—with her. At that moment, nobody was hitting her with a stick, and the sun was shining on her. In her mind, that made it a pretty nice kind of day.

"That little dog taught me a huge lesson. I use that mental image to let go of the attachment to the old,

negative tapes in my head. When I catch myself starting to replay the unhappy stuff, I stop and think of that
dog and am reminded to take her example. I think,
'Hey, cut it out . . . it's a beautiful day, and nobody's
hitting me with a stick . . . *right now.*' "

So go and enjoy the day: nobody is hitting you with
a stick right now!

Chapter Six

Life After Betrayal

A man that studieth revenge
keeps his own wounds green,
which otherwise would heal
and do well.

—Francis Bacon

Betrayals are not necessarily "events," they are often repetitive or continuous insults, hurts, and destruction. So the concept of "life goes on" simply means for some people the continuation of stress, confusion, anger, hurt, and emotional obsessiveness.

The typical scenario that I hear about on my program is the complaint of the "good kid" about what the "bad kid" can get away with—largely because right and wrong go out the window with some parents, for whom "peace at all costs" is the mantra. Of course, the cost is generally paid for by the "good kid," who has to perpetually eat dirt to survive in the family dynamic.

The errant adult child may be into drugs and/ or alcohol, one lousy relationship after another, one illegitimate child after another, one stupid financial situation after another, or may have a mean streak and spit venom wherever she or he goes. The parents, guilt-ridden by some notion of having created the monster or hell-bent on mutating the monster into a functional, decent human being, tend to bend toward the family betrayer with all kindness, financial support, and general protection. This leaves all the other family members to tread water on their own, careful not to splash the "bad kid" lest they receive the ire of the severely off-track parents.

This turns parents into betrayers of the values with which they brought up the good kids, as well as coconspirators in an ongoing hurt by ignoring and not supporting the good kids.

A similar problem occurred to one of my callers. He'd been estranged from his dad for over a year and had decided that there was no possibility that he would ever accept him back in his life. His cousin called to say the dad was dying, having maybe only a few days to a week left. The father was asking for my caller to come and see him.

When I asked about the source of an anger or emotional dissociation so strong that it could keep him away from his dying dad, he told me that his uncle, the dad's brother, had molested him over a period of about eight years when he was young. Evidently, both

Dad and Mom knew it was going on, but they never did anything to protect him, and they kept taking him over there, time after time.

Of course I was stunned to hear this and questioned why his parents would take him back there time after time. It turns out that the uncle lived with the grand-mother, who babysat him on his days off from school; his mother said if he didn't go there, she'd have to pay a babysitter.

This story gets even better—or worse, actually. When my caller, as an adult, confronted his dad, the dad told him, "We did the right thing, because if we wouldn't have done that and we'd have gotten into a fight with Grandma, then I wouldn't have inherited all the money that I got."

Wow.

Obviously, his parents were evil, wicked folks. Their betrayal of their child was motivated by greed—what more can be said about that?

My caller was being pressured by the cousin less to see the dad than to make a commitment to paying the expenses for burying him. Can you believe that? There must be some genetic anomaly in his family!

I reassured him that his parents had torn up their parent cards, and he had no moral obligation to show "compassion," nor cough up the money for a costly funeral. "I don't believe you have any moral obligation whatsoever to him—alive or dead," was my final statement to this caller.

I told him to just walk away.

There are times when you must physically and emotionally walk away. Notions of revenge, justice, comeuppance, or karma simply have to be tossed into the wind as you walk through a magical door into another realm—away from the Twilight Zone you've been in.

And that is exactly what I recommended to a woman caller who has a child with cystic fibrosis and a sister-in-law who behaves as though her child is a leper. Her own brother and parents allow the sister-in-law to dictate that this child cannot be at the grandparents' home when her child is there; nor will she allow this child into her own home. The brother and the parents want "peace," so they require my caller to be weak and meek and just conform for the sake of "family peace."

I told this caller to go over to her parents' home and let them know that if they bow to these ridiculous and mean requests from the sister-in-law, family "peace" will mean my caller has removed herself from all contact with any of them—period.

Yes, my caller was upset about "missing" her parents—but the price she has to pay for that is basically to betray her own son and treat him like an outcast to kowtow to the irrational tyranny of the sister-in-law. Betrayal often rolls downhill. I asked her to be the dam.

Is "walking away" revenge? No, I don't look at it that way at all. I see great strength and good sense in bowing out with some declaration like: "Look, I can't be around you anymore. You've hurt me so many times, and I always come back and try to make it up with you again and again. I'm too old to be stupid anymore. I just don't have room in my life for negative relationships."

It is intelligent to understand, accept, and act on the reality that this situation is like administering a slow poison to your state of mind and quality of life; walking away is dignified and strong.

There are times when getting any vengeance, or even justice, takes more from your life than it gives; bowing out is the healthiest, strongest thing to do.

One listener grew up with a father with a frightening temper. Growing up, she and her siblings were often afraid that he would snap and send one of them flying across the room. By the time she left for college, she learned that her father had had many affairs; soon afterward, her mother and father divorced.

Unbelievably, her mother encouraged her to continue a relationship with her dad; "After all, he is your father." Ugh.

So she decided to give it a try. No, he hadn't changed at all. She told him not to talk to her again, and her siblings had independently come to the same decision. That happened a decade ago.

"For about one year I mourned the loss of my father. As time went on, however, I felt that a huge burden had been lifted off my shoulders. I no longer had this destructive relationship and was free to use my energy on people who brought happiness and joy into my life.

"I didn't get vengeance or justice. I didn't need either. I don't wish him harm or sorrow. I doubt he actually has the capacity to love. Just he being him is punishment enough."

There is a lot of wisdom in this perspective, even if the betrayer doesn't "get it," and narcissistically sees himself as the one in the right. I'm sure my listener's father doesn't feel that being himself is his punishment. He is just moving on to the next person he can dominate and manipulate, and when that is settled . . . he's actually content. He is probably rationalizing the loss of his children by labeling them ungrateful, stupid, or overly connected to Mom.

My listener realized that she needed to put her energies into the quality things and people in her life today;

The best sort of revenge is not to be like him who did the injury.

—Marcus Aurelius Antoninus

to learn to be grateful for the loving relationships she does have, and not take her loved ones for granted.

The greatest source of misunderstanding for a large percentage of betrayed people is that when they stay immersed in their unhappiness about being betrayed, they in turn betray all the wonderful people who love and stand by them. Husbands and wives who spend their time depressed and anxious about their problems with a betrayer rob their families of the love and attention they would be giving them if they were not so focused on the betrayer.

Imagine digging through dirt trying to find an Oreo cookie because you are starving . . . ignoring the three-course meal on the table. That is laughable, isn't it? Well, it's not so laughable to the people who really love you, and see you constantly fussing over that one dirty cookie when they are there to offer you a veritable feast of love.

Turning your back and walking away is not an act of weakness—unless you keep slinking back. Walking away is a great act of strength, conviction, good sense, and a commitment not to let anyone bad or negative be the architect of the rest of your life. Choosing to walk away sets you free for more opportunities. New opportunities and the support of loving friends and family will recharge your emotional and physical batteries.

So many people call to ask me to explain why someone would do the kinds of things that have happened to them. From now on I will refer them to chapter 1 of this book! Suffice it to say, you cannot always explain or understand people's behaviors—although I can guess, because I'm trained as a psychotherapist. No matter what their motivations, they cannot decide for you how much power you give them over you and your life. You owe others who are important to you a commitment to accept mean behavior for what it is and to move on rather than letting it seep into what could be your good life.

One listener wrote to me of the chaos at her work situation as an office manager for a dental practice. The dentist, a friend of the family, hired her, and she joined the existing all-female staff. From day one, the other staff members were cold and unhelpful, and ultimately they caused so much grief that he let her go!

"The day after I lost the job, I was upset. I could have done a lot to discredit the dentist, but a little voice of 'Dr. Laura,' whom I have listened to for twenty-plus years, said, 'No, just do the right thing.' Take that experience, forget how cruel they were, and move on. Find a new job in an environment that will respect you and your contributions."

Yes, she probably still thought about what she could have done to get justice, some payback, some revenge, some something . . . but that would only keep her "engaged" with the situation. If you are going to leave—and leave you probably should—then do it with mind, body, and soul, not just your body.

There is a rush, a lust for quick vengeance when betrayed. I know because I have felt it every time I've been attacked. I'm glad I'm surrounded by cooler heads, people I admire and trust, who distract me with tales of new beginnings, opportunities, and challenges. It is also true that time well filled (i.e., not with obsessing) is a great salve.

In the case of a number of my betrayers, they went on to fail miserably and publicly. I know that their egos have taken a beating—but I'm not rejoicing. I simply don't care. I'm enjoying my work to a greater degree, as I am surrounded by even more support; I have taken up at least three new hobbies and am planning an incredible journey: an ocean race of six hundred miles in my forty-one-foot sailboat with a crew of six (okay . . . I'm nuts!).

When these situations first went down, of course I yearned for a bloodletting. And I actually think I would have enjoyed it at the time. Time is the smart part of life. Time reveals character. Time permits healing and growth. Time gives perspective. Time is one of life's greatest embraces.

My being has been rebooted, and while it is satisfying on some level that my betrayers ultimately failed, it gives me no surge of delight or adrenaline. I believe it went the way it should have gone, the way most of us knew it would. But if I still "cared," it would be less of me.

In other words, their loss is not my gain. My gain comes from my actions, activities, and attitude—not from their pain.

Set aside your lust for quick vengeance and continue to focus on your own path. In doing so, you solidify your reputation, character, and quality of life. Your life doesn't have to be ruled by the things that have happened to you. You can move on. You will also discover that because this challenge has occurred, you can learn and grow and become stronger.

Sometimes you discover that there is a silver lining to the whole horrid affair (see chapter 7, "Betrayal as a Blessing in Disguise?").

But before we get to the blessings that often come in the disguise of betrayals (tell me that doesn't whet your appetite!)—let me talk to you about forgiveness.

Forgiveness has the dictionary definitions of "to excuse for a fault or an offense; to pardon" and "to renounce anger or resentment against."

Forgive your enemies,
but never forget their names.

—John F. Kennedy

Let's go through these two aspects of forgiveness, one by one. First, let's look at: "to excuse for a fault or an offense; to pardon." For you Christians, forgiveness is expected in an unqualified way to restore your relationship with God and demonstrate your faith in God and Jesus Christ. For you Jews, it is not viewed as desirable to forgive people who do not repent, who do not acknowledge their responsibility, or who rationalize their behaviors. What follows is my point of view as a psychotherapist who has worked with people for over three decades.

I believe that forgiveness—in the sense of excusing—requires repentance.

Repentance includes the four R's:

1. (true) Remorse

2. (taking) Responsibility

3. (efforts to) Repair

4. (avoid) Repeating

When someone takes these four steps to heart, I believe it is quite possible to forgive and possibly have the option of reconciliation.

It is vital that right here and right now I distinguish between an "excuse" or "pardon" and renouncing anger and resentment. I believe that there are some things that are inexcusable and unforgiveable in the sense of "giving a pardon": using one's children (or any children, for that matter) for sexual pleasure and the killing of an innocent (as opposed to self-defense or defense of another) are two such examples.

In the latter situation, I would hope there was no option of reconciliation—however, renouncing anger and resentment could be tantamount to shutting the door on the betrayer so that you can get on with life, and insulating yourself from any further damage.

I leave the souls of the unforgiveable to God—it's not my place to make any pronouncement as to what I think God should do. However, I admit openly that I hope Dante's levels of hell are accurate.

Even when reconciliation is possible or advisable, quick forgiveness is not a healthy thing to do. I have found in my professional experience that people need to come to that place, forgiveness, through a lot of small towns. Believe it or not, because of shock and denial, it takes some people a bit of traveling time before they come to the place of even being concretely aware and recognizing the fact that they have been "done bad." They then have to run by the road signs of hurt, grief, and anger and have the rightness and reasonableness of these feelings validated. It is amazing to me how many people have difficulty acknowledging that they have been hurt while they are simultaneously obviously suffering, and their lives are totally off track.

Once folks accept the reality of what has happened, they naturally turn to desires for justice or restitution. When those are not feasible, the hurt starts all over again. It is at that point that I often tell them that although their feelings are natural, valid, reasonable, understandable, normal, healthy, and quite human—they have to let it go and move on to the rest of their lives.

Pardoning someone who seems to really mean that they are sorry does not mean that you have to reconcile without many strings attached. Letting go of anger is good for blood pressure and stomach acid. Continuing a relationship with that individual may not be advisable.

Reconciliation is a far more burdensome enterprise for a wrongdoer than even repentance entails. Repentance is a necessary but insufficient part of the process of reconciliation. There has to be rehabilitation and a serious rebuilding of trust. Unfortunately, betrayers often tire quickly of efforts at rehabilitation and the interminable requirement to rebuild trust and minister to the pain they've caused. They usually get impatient and require that the injured party just "forgive (excuse) and forget."

News flash: that means that they haven't changed two iotas.

Keep in mind that you may never see fit to pardon or excuse no matter how often they and others pressure you; and you sure aren't ever obligated to reconcile if that puts you anywhere close to harm's way or continued insult or hurt.

You are not a bad person if you don't forgive—because, as I said, some things are just not forgivable. Not pardoning or excusing does not mean that you can't let go. You can most definitely not give the betrayer any quarter, nor those supporting him or her, and still just let go. When I work with some people on my radio program I give them one of several images to help them with the process of letting go without pardoning or excusing the betrayer's wrongdoing, if that is not possible.

One image is to put all their anger, hurt, resentment, and vengeful feelings in balloons—with their qualities the same as helium. Now I have them imagine letting these balloons go to float ever away, one by one, until they are left in peace in the lovely sunshine of a new day.

Generally, people are heard to cry softly and then sigh deeply—physical evidence of an emotional burden being lifted off their shoulders.

You can also think of burying all those horrible feelings in a box in your backyard, or writing a letter to that betrayer and then burning it in your fireplace and letting the smoke of the whole situation waft up the chimney, diffusing into oblivion. Whichever image or technique most works for you, this ritual of letting go works when you are ready to move on.

And move on you must, because, as I said earlier, to press the "pause" button on your life by staying stuck in rage and hurt is to become complicit with your betrayer in destroying your life.

It is always interesting to note how folks respond to situations of betrayal.

A recent very public case of betrayal is Tiger Woods and the multiple affairs he indulged in while presenting himself as a stand-up guy. An interesting poll appeared on foxnews.com. The question was asked: "Do you think Tiger should be forgiven"? Here are the results:

1. Twenty-four percent said, "Yes. He's human. He made a mistake. Time to move on."

2. Twenty-seven percent said, "Maybe. It's really up to his wife and family."

3. Twenty-seven percent said, "No. He wronged his family, fans, and sponsors. He will always be a jerk."

4. Twenty percent said, "I don't really care. Hello? He's a golfer!"

Let's go through these responses one by one:

1. "Mistake." He didn't make a mistake. A mistake is taking the wrong golf shoes. His was a pattern, a long-term behavior of screwing around with babes wherever he went.

2. "Wife/family." He didn't just betray his marital vows and his relationship with his children. Other people's children were directed by their trusting parents to consider him a role model of discipline, family values, and character. His sponsors used his image to project something dignified to their potential and actual customers.

3. "Jerk." This we can't know. The level of his public humiliation, his loss of sponsorships and income, and the threat of losing his wife and children may have been enough stress to humble his arrogance and ego. Only God and his wife will know the true depth of his repentance and commitments to others.

4. "Golfer." No—he was more than a golfer—he was an image of a hero. He reaped the rewards of this "image" and had a responsibility to continue actually earning it.

I was the most curious about the 20 percent in group 4 who didn't think this mattered at all. These folks always concern me—they appear in families, communities, and work situations. They have the belief that values and morals don't matter as long as "something" is being done: be it the manufacture of widgets, government policies they like, or the excitement of a sport. These people are a gross disappointment to the rest of us who wish to have things matter; who wish to have the actions of people matter more than their entertainment value; who wish to believe that the actions of all human beings impact others, and for that they must have a sense of responsibility.

The moral of the Tiger Woods story is that betrayals are always far-reaching, whether or not you are in the public eye. We each have the opportunity to do the right thing in spite of impulse, greed, opportunity, temptations, or any other emotion that needs to be disciplined for the greater good.

However, there are people who are simply bad; people who don't mind hurting good people or other bad people. If there is one lesson to be learned from this whole book, it is this: You will be betrayed. I have two words for you: NOW WHAT?

Being betrayed was not in your control. NOW WHAT is in your control.

Chapter Seven

Betrayal as a Blessing in Disguise?

Without a trace of irony I can say I have been blessed with brilliant enemies. I owe them a great debt, because they redoubled my energies and drove me in new directions.

—E. O. Wilson

I really can't believe it. I got up at 5:30 a.m. to have a quick breakfast and sit down to write this chapter, and found out I was betrayed. My heart is still pounding.

A few years ago I let someone go from my boat crew. I didn't go public with it. I didn't embarrass this person. I just stopped inviting this person to participate. Recently something nice was posted about me on an Internet sailing site, and after a few days, up pops a very snarky comment by him about my abilities. I sat here stunned; I had been publicly protective of his loutish behavior, and look at my reward. But considering what I think of his character, to "take his shot" to repair his ego—even after all of this time—seemed like something I should not be surprised about.

I sent a personal and private text message to him saying that what he did was nasty—and left it at that.

He immediately shot back a text message, which I deleted without reading. It didn't matter what he'd said—it probably wasn't any nicer than his public post. And frankly, I didn't care. I'd rather be me being *classy* than him being *nasty.*

This book is the most autobiographical of any book I've ever written . . . following closely after the public revelations of my childhood in *Bad Childhood— Good Life.* Because of the unpleasant parental dynamics of my childhood, I've always been a bit hypersensitive to criticism and suspicious about love and affection. I have worked my way through much of this slowly and painfully throughout my six decades of life.

Because of my personal struggles and professional training, I have an acute understanding and compassion for the suffering of others. Although I began my educational career leading toward being a biological scientist, my true vocation came and got me: psychotherapist and talk-show host who, for over three decades, helps millions deal with the inner and outer turmoil that is a large part of life. I help people let go of one side of the swimming pool so they *can* get to the other side of the pool—without drowning; but maybe with some uncomfortable gulps of ill-tasting water.

Most of my education did not come from schoolin' nor readin'—it came from talking to real people going through real situations and struggling to find real solutions five days a week, three hours a day, for almost three and a half decades.

As I matured, so did my insight and abilities. Figuring out how to help people over the years has taught me so much in my personal life that has been benevolent and beneficial. Talking to women I identify with who are facing terminal cancer and have small children; talking to men who've lost everything and crawl their way back . . . all of this has helped me appreciate my life, opportunities, and blessings so much more.

When I'm in a funk, all I have to do is turn on the microphone at twelve noon Pacific time, and I am immersed in the world of others who need me—the best medicine for coming out of yourself. The appreciation I receive from listeners and callers is a daily reminder that I do matter . . . and I'm not "stupid," like my father usually told me.

Purpose is the greatest motivator for a love of life— which is why I will only retire posthumously!

The blessing in disguise for all the betrayals I have experienced is the awareness and knowledge to write this book to help you deal with one of the most fundamental realities of life: there are bad people ready to hurt good people, for fun, for ego, for notice, for any damn reason they muster up in the shadow of their puny character and conscience.

Now let me get to other things to learn from the disaster of betrayal and how to identify the silver lining. Blessings often come in disguise, and the purpose of this chapter is to open your mind and heart to the blessing. If you are so bogged down with hurt and rage over a betrayal, then you might miss out on what could possibly change your life forever—and in the most positive way.

One young woman wrote me that she and her husband were planning their wedding, paying for and planning it all by themselves. As they had modest means financially, they decided they would prefer a small ceremony with only close friends and family. His family hit the roof. They demanded that distant relatives (unknown to the couple) should be invited, and went so far as to invite those relatives themselves! The parents then got on the phone and contacted the rest of his family to join their team and take a stand against what his father called the couple's "disloyalty and lack of human compassion." The groom's father, through an e-mail no less, told them they were no longer members of his family anymore, since they wouldn't do it his way.

It seems unbelievable that a parent would act so harshly for such a small reason. It was devastating for my listener's fiancé. They felt totally alone. They never in their wildest dreams could have imagined that level of betrayal coming from their closest family members. Neither of them had ever felt emotional pain and isolation on that level.

They initially dealt with it with a lot of crying and talking. Now, two years later, they don't dwell on it anymore, even though it is still at the back of their minds. They didn't retaliate, and some of his family made amends with them, which helped them to move on. Nothing makes everything all better, though. Some things can't be undone or unsaid. They are accepting the reality of a split family . . . all because they wanted a small ceremony.

The blessing? It should be obvious! It is a blessing that the split from his punitive, controlling, and demanding father happened sooner rather than later. The young couple would have been miserable for years, attempting to fence with his controlling father. His parents would have tried to coerce them into all sorts of unpleasant circumstances until the end of time. None of that is a factor now. "We can live peacefully in that regard," she wrote.

While it is sad to have a family split or break down, sometimes it is salvation staring you in the face. If her husband had been weak or defensive, there would have been a major blood war, or maybe no marriage at all. That he was strong and honest enough to acknowledge the tyranny that was his family, and cleave only to her, is the blessing for her. She found herself a real man.

There are times in one's life when moving on is so obviously a good plan. But people get afraid of change and challenge; the unfamiliar is insecure, and therefore frightening. So people stay too long in circumstances they shouldn't, and pay the price emotionally and often physically through health problems caused by stress.

One woman wrote about a newly promoted coworker who, for her own reasons, behaved in a manner that indicated that she felt inadequate for the new job and threatened by the greater experience of some around her, namely my listener. She began competing with my listener by false accusations to superiors and hoarding information necessary for my listener to do her job.

My listener started tiptoeing around this coworker because she was afraid of the next stab in the back. She was always on her guard. She withdrew a bit and gave the coworker more control in hopes she would be left alone. Going to a supervisor did not help; he just said, "Work it out."

She ended up getting pneumonia and had to spend three weeks at home, trying to recuperate. She knew it was her work situation that was causing her weakened physical condition . . . and she relapsed three months later.

It was at this point that she realized it was a life-or-death situation. She applied for other jobs. She ended up with one that had more benefits, better hours, and more opportunities to go on business trips paid by the company. And when she goes on those trips, she remembers that it is because her coworker made her miserable that she decided to switch jobs.

"I probably wouldn't have made the switch otherwise," she wrote. People get comfortable and stop looking for better opportunities until circumstances jettison them out of their complacency. While her former job was okay, in the same building and on another floor was this better one.

I think she should send the ex-coworker a thank-you note . . . only in her mind. If she really sent one, as an act of vengeance, it would just turn the nasty spigot back on, and her ex-coworker would try to undermine her where she was now. It is a far, far better thing she does to not see this woman and not think about her—no precious life time should be spent looking back on manure once the flowers bloom.

Life's lessons are valuable, and not just to be rued or feared. One listener's earliest memory of being betrayed was by her best friend in junior high school. It was the summer the friend had invited her to spend time with her family, beach camping. She was all ready to go until a few days before the trip, when the friend told her that her parents had decided to not have friends come.

Later she learned that her "best friend" had invited another friend. She felt crushed. "It was then when I started having trouble trusting people."

Well, that's not exactly the whole story. She also wrote about her parents divorcing, and remarriages that ended up with Brady Bunch scenarios, not as humorous and peaceful as the television series.

Clearly, in the midst of all that family turmoil and confused bonds and loyalties, having her "best friend"—whom she depended on for constancy and security—betray her was the last straw.

"I became very angry and emotionally unavailable. I got vengeance by never speaking with her again. I just dumped friends for every reason in the book. If I didn't like one tiny thing about them, I just never called them back, or I ignored them."

And this latter mode is often where people stay stuck for their whole lives: in purgatory; somewhere between punishing everybody and protecting themselves. I talk to people who have made this choice to stay revolving around the same hurt for the totality of their lives; sad and useless.

Fortunately, this listener learned that there are different types of friends and family, and she shouldn't put maximum expectations on all of them because that leads directly into disappointment and hurt. Of course, as a teenager who was not in control of all the changes in her life due to the shenanigans of the adults playing musical chairs with kids and spouses, one cannot expect the revelations she would have as a more mature adult.

"I seem to expect too much from people," she said. "I need to trust my instincts, love people for who they are and be wise about what I share with whom; but also realize that nobody's perfect, and I will always be disappointed with something, because people are all imperfect."

It is this sort of wisdom that I extol every day on my program. I talk about concentric circles around you: there are those from whom you can expect and receive more than those in the outer rings of Saturn. There are some people you play tennis or badminton or cards and chat about silly things with (and that is fun), and there are those you turn to when tragedy strikes or you are needful of profound support.

It is most important to be able to distinguish between those rings and appreciate each person for what he or she is able to do and give. This requires maturity, which is most often forged in the fire of emotional pain: betrayals.

Betrayals can teach you—if you're listening—to allow people their faults and strengths and to use your own judgment to determine where to place each individual in your solar system.

Immaturity leads you to just assume everybody will take care of you because you simply want it and need it. Maturity leads you to make your choices wisely.

When I mention "immaturity," I don't mean that in a bad way—it is not condescension. I only mean that life experiences combined with a willing and open substrate yield an understanding that allows you the opportunity to make choices that are self-constructive versus self-destructive.

Maturity gives you perspective and the security to make assessments necessary to protect yourself and get the best results when dealing with people. People are unpredictable, not transparent. It is important that you

*E*ach friend represents a
world in us, a world possibly
not born until they arrive, and it
is only by this meeting that
a new world is born.

—Anaïs Nin

internalize your experiences so that you can use them as a basis of judgment.

Trusting everybody is foolish and opens you up to becoming a victim. Such naïveté is not charming, sweet, advisable, or smart. Being willing to put aside your dearest hopes, dreams, and knee-jerk emotional needs to take the time to assess a problematic relationship at an earlier stage is an important aspect to having a good life.

Usually one of the first questions I ask when people call me with their relationship concerns is, "When did you first notice this behavior?" First, a lot of people lie because they're embarrassed that they ignored Vesuvius erupting from day one. Second, they try to minimize by saying, "Well, it wasn't so bad." Third, they attempt to sound magnanimous by saying, "Well, I wanted to give him/her the time to change."

Ultimately the true answer is, "I wanted this/him/her to just be the right thing/person for me so bad that I just rushed forward." And the result is usually a betrayal, as the person or situation in question has not been appropriately vetted. This turns out to be coconspiracy of betrayal; in part, you brought it upon yourself.

A few rude awakenings with betrayals of fidelity or finances, and hopefully you will get the message that if you want your life to simply unfold totally smoothly without your vigilance and discernment (judgments happening from the eyebrows up)—fuggedaboutit.

Sometimes the blessing from betrayal is just a surprise. One door closes and another opens—so keep your eyes and heart open. One listener found out her husband and a friend's wife were having an affair. She met with the friend so they could help each other deal with this incredible betrayal.

Well, well, well . . . they each became the other's sounding board and friend; they helped each other with the children; and before you knew it, they'd developed a love relationship. They ended up getting married and have raised three children to be responsible adults and share one granddaughter.

"It has been the kind of marriage that I always dreamed of—we are perfect for each other and have enjoyed twenty-two years of marriage. It is a beautiful life."

They didn't come together to hurt their philandering spouses—they came together with innocent and honest hopes of helping their children cope well with this betrayal and disaster. In doing so—coming from a place of goodness—they discovered each other. Lovely story—probably not typical—but lovely nonetheless.

When goodness follows the betrayal, people are more drawn to you, and your opportunities for healthy support and surprising events are more likely!

Of course, you have to cope with the initial urge to confront betrayers, take 'em out, read 'em down, blow 'em up. As the quip goes, "Don't get into a fight with a pig, because they love rolling around in the mud!"

It takes some finesse to learn how to confront evil so as not to self-destruct by giving betrayers more power to hurt you. On the other hand, it is gruesome to imagine just letting it all go without there being some acknowledgment of their wrongdoing, and some consequence.

Meanness and evil live off conflict—it makes them feel justified in some warped, twisted, backward, inside-out way. When they're confronted with who they are and what they've done, they are usually brilliant in finding a way to turn it around and make themselves victims.

When one of my betrayers was slapped down verbally by a number of independent people bored and annoyed with her continued harassment of me, her response was to claim that I paid people to criticize her . . . poor thing. She made herself the victim. Delusional at worst; clever at best.

That is an example of what happens when betrayers are confronted, and their little perfect picture of invulnerability is besmirched. So be careful. Even when what you're throwing is water, some splashes back on you.

However, it is a blessing when people come to your defense, even when it has absolutely no impact whatsoever on the bad guy/gal. That is the blessing in disguise: that others are willing to make a statement and stand by you and/or what is right. It may change absolutely nothing in the situation, but you need to embrace that goodness that trickled out of it. Reward it with gratitude—it means you are not alone, and somebody cares.

Be aware that most "standers by" may not go all the way and shun or punish the evildoer—everybody has their limits based on their own agenda and how much they are potentially willing to sacrifice. Don't judge the amount of support. Embrace whatever comes your way—it is all in the category of blessing.

In doing all of the above, looking for the silver lining, you learn how not to feel the victim. If you are grasping on to that identity, you marinate in unhappiness and resentment at every turn. That is masochism—don't do it.

And if what has happened to you makes you question yourself—that is a blessing also! Just like a pilot walks

*I*f you are going through hell, keep going.

—Winston Churchill

around the plane and kicks the tires before he takes off, you should walk around yourself and kick yourself now and then to make sure you are doing and being your best. There are likely some things you've done or said that had the misfortune of moving the ugly situation into being. While that doesn't make you responsible for the sick actions of others, it should make you assess yourself, your motives and actions, and be more circumspect about even your off-the-cuff comments or knee-jerk reactions.

I know I have regrets in that department. My weakness comes in wanting the fairy tale of being rescued from the dragons. And while some of that has occurred in my life (gotta love when it does), that is usually only one part of what makes life go on in a happy way. Support is an inspiration, not a panacea. Support helps you feel that there is still hope in trying and moving on. Support is a blessing—don't turn up your nose at it, no matter how small the gesture.

Afterword

There is no reason why good cannot triumph as often as evil. The triumph of anything is a matter of organization. If there are such things as angels, I hope that they are organized along the lines of the Mafia.

—Kurt Vonnegut

The most recent incident, still fresh in my mind, occurred in August 2010. A black woman called me asking for help with her white husband's friends. As I do with each call, I asked for specifics to determine whether her husband and his friends were behaving inappropriately or whether she was simply hypersensitive about the racial situation.

Her first example was that his friends ask her for a "black perspective" on things, as though there were always a stereotypical answer. The exact phrase she used was "what do blacks think" about certain issues. I commented that in my opinion, this was not inappropriate or insulting, as they simply wanted to know her perspective as a black woman. She then went on to tell me that they use the N-word and asked me if that was wrong to do in her presence. I responded with the point that it would appear this was an issue of context, as many black musicians, actors, producers, writers, singers, and comedians use the word liberally and many black men use the word affectionately with each other.

That clearly wasn't what she expected to hear, though, as she went ballistic on me, and the call degenerated from there. I was trying to make an important point about context, and she took offense. I realized I had made a mistake. In my attempt to help her, I offended her and others for whom that word is anathema. I pulled myself off the air, wrote an apology, and issued it the next morning. And then I waited. And waited.

Forty-eight hours after I had made the mistake, and thirty-six hours after I had released my apology, I was suddenly and vehemently attacked for my mistake. It all exploded into wall-to-wall CNN coverage as well as the number one international story on Google News: Dr. Laura said the N-word eleven times.

That I never called anyone the epithet went unnoticed.

That I apologized, immediately and without anyone's prompting, for hurting anyone—however unintentional—went largely unnoticed.

That I was labeled a racist bigot all over the Internet and media—went quite noticed.

In today's mainstream media, context does not matter. People like me are censured and threatened with censorship not because of what we say, but because of what special interest group we have offended.

In 2008, Jesse Jackson called President Obama "an f-ing half-breed N," but no one called for boycotts against Jesse and his programs. Bill Maher—on *Larry King Live* this past September—accused Newt Gingrich of calling Obama "a code word" for N—and he said the word full out as I did, yet Bill Maher was not criticized by the media at all, and no one called for HBO to cancel his show.

But I made a factual statement—blacks use the N-word in a variety of contexts—and you would think I was the reincarnation of John Wayne Gacy.

So on Thursday, August 12, 2010, thirty-six hours after my apology, *Media Matters*, the Urban League, the NAACP, and others began a campaign to harass my affiliates and sponsors. Mind you: I never called anyone a name. Rather, I was pointing out the circumstances under which it is used. But I was white using a word that many blacks use all the time. In the PC world of special interest groups looking for a power edge, funding, and attention, I became a bigger target than the KKK.

The shark frenzy was astounding: sheer blood-lust to demonize a woman with no history of racism whatsoever after three decades on the air. My long-standing record of support for couples involved in interracial dating and marriage: that didn't matter. My support for interracial adoption: that didn't matter, either. None of that mattered—it was yet another moment for special interest groups and activists to raise a fist to prove they are victims.

That Friday afternoon, sitting at my desk still amazed at the overreaction, I decided I was done. Every few years some group gets all furious at something I have said and goes after my show's affiliates and sponsors. They demand that my advertisers stop sponsoring my show and they demand that my affiliates cancel me. Basically, they issue an all-points bulletin to silence my voice.

Once I told a mom of a profoundly autistic child who had tendencies toward violence to find a bonded babysitter with special training, buy a new dress, and go to a family party with her husband and just have a nice time. Whoa! You'd have thought I told her to leave him in the desert. Another time a woman called about a child with Tourette's that was out of control and was wondering if this child should come to a wedding ceremony. I said no because I thought it was unfair to disturb the wedding. You'd again have thought I told her to leave this child in the desert. There was the issue of gay marriage, over which I was branded as "antigay," even though I am for gay domestic partnerships. And the issue of a mother concerned about her high-school daughter's field trip to a mosque soon after 9/11. I suggested she determine if there was any jihad rhetoric in this mosque first, just to be safe, but that led to more outcry. . . . Anyway, on and on it has gone.

My show's sponsors are family people who need to make a living. Even when sponsors are sympathetic to me, if they are threatened with economic destruction, they have to walk away for a while. Affiliates enjoy a certain amount of attention-grabbing controversy—but ferocious daily harassment for supporting "evil" can get to be a bit much, as daily business is disrupted. When I take all this together—my constantly being vilified, and my sponsors' being harassed—I feel I am in the position of having to withhold an opinion simply because some people don't agree with it. Ultimately, I am not able to enjoy freedom of speech, because our culture has turned from debate to eliminating contrary speech.

That morning, when I decided I was done, I did not mean that I was done helping people deal with morals, values, ethics, and principles . . . but I did mean that terrestrial radio was no longer the way to go. I made an announcement on August 17 on *Larry King Live* that

December 31, 2010, would be my last day on terrestrial radio. Immediately, many in the radio industry called me and told me just to "wait it out" and then get on with my program. I understood that the storm would pass, but I was tired of the threats to be shut down. I am not the only one attacked and threatened with having my First Amendment rights stripped from me for saying something controversial or having an opinion. Just in the past six months, Rick Sanchez was fired from CNN for stating an opinion that offended some people. Juan Williams was fired from NPR for giving his own honest perspective of life post-9/11. Leroy Towns, a law professor at the University of North Carolina, said in a blog about me: "The right of free speech is being replaced by The Right Not To Be Offended."

So on August 17, I shocked the world and announced my decision to leave terrestrial radio. The next day, THAT was the number one story in the world on Google News. And I haven't wavered one millimeter from my decision.

On the morning of August 18, the head of talk programming for Sirius XM called and asked, "How would you like to move your voice to the pro-free-speech world of satellite radio?"

It was a very wise person who said that when one door closes, another opens. It was time for me to make a change, to shake up my life, to take on new endeavors—and this shark attack was a blessing in disguise, as so many are. In addition to satellite radio, all kinds of alternative media and communications folks have contacted me, and we have been dealing with new opportunities. I will be writing children's books as an app, we already have a Dr. Laura's Moral Compass app, I am on satellite radio for six hours a day, I have what I think is a terrific television idea, and more book ideas come to mind every day. I feel released, free, reinvigorated. I am proud of myself for taking a stand. I will be able to say my piece without threats to sponsors, affiliates, or my livelihood. If people disagree, they are welcome to forward their perspective—I hope without personal attacks, rage, and hatred.

I am very happy. I have survived so many shark attacks and each time I've simply regrouped—or as Sarah Palin texted me, "reloaded"—and had new and better experiences and adventures. I no longer fear shark attacks. I don't enjoy them, but I know that after the bloodletting, it's up to me to make it a blessing and not a burden.

Postscript

I loved writing this book—absolutely adored every minute of it. I've managed to purge myself of some ugly junk inside my head and heart, and I've come to recognize how wonderfully far I've come in dealing better and better with betrayals.

At this point, they are both a sense of humor and a personal challenge.

Character, as one of my listeners wrote, is forged in the furnace of difficulty and trials. There is no way in this life that you can always prevent feeling hurt or being harmed. Too many people spend too much of their precious time and energy trying to do just that. Take that time and energy and focus on building yourself, so that you will be able to handle the slings and arrows of life.

Do not press the "pause" button on your life by festering with anger and feelings of vengeance; all we each have is time, so fill it well.

I still love the concept of revenge—and always will. I just love the concept of enjoying my life more.

And to those who have ever betrayed me—or will—I have this to say: "Frankly, my dears, I don't give a damn."

HARPER LUXE

THE NEW LUXURY IN READING

We hope you enjoyed reading
our new, comfortable print size and found it
an experience you would like to repeat.

Well – you're in luck!

HarperLuxe offers the finest in fiction and
nonfiction books in this same larger print size and
paperback format. Light and easy to read, HarperLuxe
paperbacks are for book lovers who want to see
what they are reading without the strain.

For a full listing of titles and
new releases to come, please visit our website:

www.HarperLuxe.com